THE BANDITS OF CISTERNA

THE
BANDITS
OF CISTERNA

by
WILLIAM PICKERING MM
and
ALAN HART

11th. Jan. 1993

*To Bob & Marjorie Clark, Colleagues of No.1 Special
Force during happy days spent at Monopoli.
With very best wishes,*
Bill Pickering

LEO COOPER
LONDON

First published in Great Britain in 1991 by
LEO COOPER
190 Shaftesbury Avenue, London WC2H 8JL
an imprint of Pen & Sword Books Ltd,
47 Church Street, Barnsley, S. Yorks S70 2AS

Copyright © William Pickering MM and Alan Hart, 1991

A CIP catalogue record for this book
is available from the British Library

ISBN 0 85052 333 8

Printed in Great Britain by
Redwood Press Limited, Melksham, Wiltshire

To the memory of the late
CAPTAIN JOHN KEANY
of Cork, Eire and of the late
MAJOR ADRIAN HOPE
of South Africa,
both dedicated officers of
the Special Operations Executive
who gave their lives
in the noble cause
of freedom;
also to my fallen comrades
from the irrepressible
Partisans of North-West Italy.
It was a privilege to serve
with you.

CONTENTS

ACKNOWLEDGMENTS

I would like to thank the many people who have helped me with the research and preparation of this book, especially Lieutenant-Colonel Max Salvadori D.S.O. M.C., Professor of Smith College, Massachusetts, U.S.A; Chris Woods, of Special Forces Club, London; Settimo Maggiorino, Mondovi, and Pietro Berruti of Barbaresco, Peidmont, Italy; the late Basil O. Temple (ex U.S.A.A.F.), of New Orleans, U.S.A., Len Kelsall and Harry Hargreaves (ex S.O.E. operators).

I am also grateful to Peter Morrall, of the George and Dragon Hotel, Cheadle, Cheshire, and John Smith, of Special Forces Club, who accompanied Alan Hart and myself on our research and photographic tours of North-West Italy.

I am indebted to Malcolm Munthe for permission to quote from his book, *Sweet in War* (Duckworth, 1954).

FOREWORD
By
Professor Max Salvadori

'Quick! Germans are close!' − to the best of my memory
this is what I heard when parachuted in the early hours of 5
February, 1945. Thanks very much! Deep in snow, with all
the equipment I carried I couldn't move. Happily, next to
me within a few seconds appeared Bill Pickering, barely
more than half my age, strong, agile and, above all, cheerful. Unforgettable help for which I have ever since been
grateful. He got me out of the snow and led me to Captain
Ballard, head of the 'reception committee'.

My destination was Milan, HQ of the clandestine Committee of National Liberation in Italy's occupied enemy territory. Couriers were to maintain contact with John Keany
and Bill, instructed to remain in uniform in Partisan-con-
trolled areas: it didn't work.

When the 'chute opened and the fall became a measured
descent, silence was compete in the darkness of the starry
night. The mind raced, summarizing the past, planning for
the immediate future. This was the 66th month of the war −
last chapter for me in the exhausting twenty-odd years of
anti-fascist militancy in countries of three continents. During
the 66 months nothing had given me more satisfaction than
to enlist in the U.K. armed forces, joining Britons, Comm-
onwealth Britishers and other tens of thousands who fought
(and many died) valiantly. Alone among the Allies to have
fought since the inception of the war, through their tenacity,
spirit of sacrifice and firm commitment, enemy victories had
not become *Victory,* Resistance movements had had time to

get organized, Russians to regroup, Americans to make ready. War was now getting close to the end but there was still much to do, plenty of time to die. All contributed to VE and VJ Day, but I was well aware that from May, 1940, to the Autumn of 1942 the still greater armed conflict was primarily a duel between satanic Nazis supported worldwide by hordes of allies, clients and admirers, and democratic Britons who stoically endured suffering and losses, and never became discouraged — the likes of S.O.E. personnel of all ranks who died while helping Resistance fighters, of Bill Pickering who miraculously survived and whom we thank for having given us this truthful account of his war experiences.

Max Salvadori, DSO, MC

PREFACE

In September, 1943, the Italian Government of Marshal Badoglio surrendered to the invading Allied Forces. This decision to capitulate was not recognized by the occupying German troops who continued to try to control central and northern Italy. The Fascist dictator Mussolini was evacuated north of the Gothic Line where he remained in command of the Republican Army.

The Allied invasion of Sicily, the Salerno landings and the forming of the beachhead at Anzio were not the only pressures brought to bear on the Axis powers. Throughout Italy, anti-Fascist Partisans formed resistance groups to harass and disrupt the Nazi war effort.

Their guerrilla tactics were a constant thorn in the side of the occupying troops, but back in Allied headquarters it was decided that this splendid work needed the additional attribute of concerted action.

Winston Churchill, who wanted to set Europe ablaze with resistance to Hitler, had been the prime mover in the formation of a secret force known as the Special Operations Executive. They had already shown their mettle by coordinating the brave resistance to the Nazi occupiers of mainland Europe. Now they were called in again to create the maximum disruption of the Axis war machine as it retreated step by bloody step from Italy.

And so it was that at 2 o'clock on a crisp, moonlit morning on 4 February, 1945, six men of the S.O.E. parachuted 100 miles behind enemy lines into the Piedmont province of Italy.

The secret six came from Britain, Ireland, the U.S.A., South Africa and Italy. Their orders were to link up with a group of Partisans known and feared by the Nazis as 'The Bandits of Cisterna'.

One of those parachutists was a 21-year-old Sergeant from the Royal Corps of Signals named Bill Pickering. This is his story.

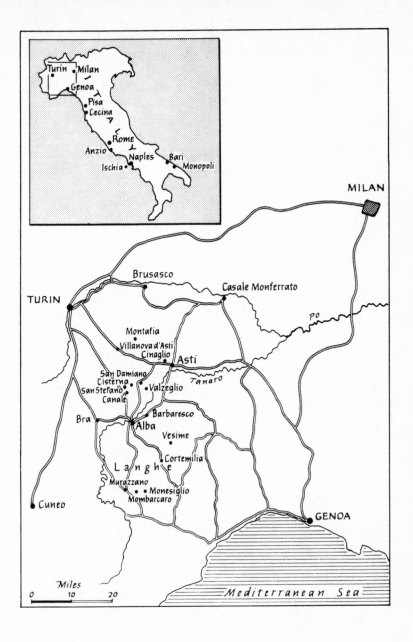

I

ON OUR WAY

As we filed haphazardly across the grassy fields of the temporary American air base at Cecina, near Pisa, our team was in high spirits. For months we had been preparing for this moment, so our relief at being on our way at last outweighed any apprehension as we crossed the makeshift runway towards the U.S. Air Force Dakota.

I was still bearing a scar on my forehead above the left eye from a fight the night before. It was a souvenir of a drunken evening which ended in an all-too-familiar shambles with a scrap between a fellow sergeant and myself.

The following morning, as I licked my wounds and nursed a hangover, we heard that our operation was to start that night. The meteorologists were forecasting a clear, moonlit sky with the strong possibility of snow at our dropping point. That was a mixed blessing. On the one hand we were likely to have a soft landing. On the other there was the added danger of hitting an unseen tree or plunging into a snow-covered pond.

Our adrenalin was pumping at maximum speed as we climbed the steps and entered the empty fuselage of the plane. It was a DC3 Dakota, normally used to drop supplies, in standard camouflage colours with white American stars on each of the wingtips.

The six of us had each been offered and had each declined suicide tablets to swallow in the event of capture. But I did carry a comb with a hidden saw inside it and a compass which was concealed inside a button of my tunic. Less subtle amongst my armaments were the Marlin sub-machine gun, the Colt 45 automatic pistol and the Commando fighting knife.

The knife, with its eight-inch blade, was in a sheath strapped to my left hip. The pistol was in its holster on my right hip. The Marlin was slung across my back. Fortunately my wireless transmitter and hand generator had already been stored on board to be dropped separately. Otherwise I would have buried myself on impact and they would have needed an excavator to dig me out.

Under my dark grey flying suit, I wore the traditional battledress of khaki shirt and trousers over Army issue Y-fronts and grey socks. For good luck I had given an extra polish to my size 7½ black boots. This fetching ensemble was completed with a dark rubber helmet which covered head, ears and neck, exposing just my face and hands to the elements.

My comrades were similarly armed to the teeth. Our leader was Major Max Salvadori, a 35-year-old Italian who had already won the Military Cross two years earlier. Major Max was decorated for his daring exploits prior to the Anzio landings. He had crossed the Garigliano River north of Naples with other agents at the considerable risk of possible painful torture and certain death if captured.

Now he was leading another band of men behind enemy lines. Soldiers cannot elect their leaders, but I could think of nobody I would have rather followed in such a situation. As an impetuous youngster, my greatest fear was to show any fear. I had no way of knowing how many of my colleagues felt the same way. I only knew that this handsome major inspired a quiet confidence in me that led to cautious optimism in the outcome of the mission.

Major Max was six feet tall, with brown hair and striking pale blue eyes. He sported a military moustache of the type favoured by Errol Flynn, Clark Gable and other Hollywood stars who represented the swashbuckling school of acting. He came from the Marche region of Italy, near Ancona, and had served a prison sentence prior to the outbreak of war because of his anti-Fascist views. Fluent in Italian of course, the Major also spoke impeccable English with an educated, public-school accent.

Second-in-command of our group was Major Adrian Hope, a quietly-spoken Colonial type whose son Billy was fighting with the South African Army. Major Adrian was a middle-aged caricature of a soldier from Johannesburg, who talked to us in the clipped tones of the B.B.C. radio announcers.

It was a source of great amusement to our Partisan hosts that he brought the same precise diction into his attempts at Italian. I have never known any man before or since who could make the colourful Italian language sound so unmistakeably English.

Major Adrian was also a tall figure, perhaps not as athletically-built as our leader, but he still managed to exude authority from his slim, upright frame. The Partisans grew to love him. They thought he was a typical English gentleman and it was easy to imagine him as 'something in the city' — walking along Threadneedle Street in pin-striped suit, bowler hat and carrying a rolled black umbrella.

If Major Hope was the quiet man of our group, then Captain John Keany was undoubtedly the talkative one. He was a public-school-educated Irishman with only the faintest hint of a brogue. Aged 28, he was a powerfully-built man in his prime, standing 5 feet 10 inches tall with brown hair and blue eyes.

Captain Keany had joined the Royal Irish Fusiliers at the outbreak of hostilities and had no intention of letting Ireland's neutrality stand between him and the thrills of battle. He was courageous to a fault, wanting to engage and fight the enemy at every opportunity. He had a terrific sense of humour and was the life and soul of our party.

Perhaps I am being unkind to suggest that the good Captain was a natural warrior who would have been equally at home fighting for the Germans against the British. It was the good fortune of the Allies that he decided to espouse their cause and give them his unswerving loyalty.

3

I was one of three radio operators in the group. The other two were Giovanni, an American of Italian extraction who was a member of the Office of Strategic Services, and Corporal 'Busty' Millard.

Giovanni was a quiet 26-year-old from New York who spoke fluent Italian. His English had a strong Bronx accent. Although he was only small, Giovanni had proved in training that he could not be underestimated. There was an air of quiet menace about him which made you aware that this was not a man to be crossed.

He had been seconded to the S.O.E. team temporarily from the O.S.S. because he was heading for the same area. But Giovanni was essentially a hitch-hiker who went his own way after the big drop.

Corporal Millard was 28 and a Regular Army man who had served in India before the war. Busty – so called because of his ample bosom – stood 5 feet 6 inches tall with dark curly hair. He was an affable character who liked nothing better than a pub crawl with the boys.

It always puzzled me that a man like Millard had found himself in the S.O.E. He never struck me as being adventurous or exceptionally patriotic – just one of the lads. He probably thought the same about me!

In those days I had blond hair and the figure of a keen sportman who loved soccer, rugby and hockey, but whose love of beer had put something of a strain on his waistline. I was the baby of the group at just 21 years old, but I possessed the bravado of a cocky kid for whom life had become one great big adventure.

My earlier exploits had given me a limited command of the Italian language, but not enough to fool the natives or the Gestapo. However, being an impetuous youth with an illogical belief in my own immortality, such considerations never clouded my thoughts for long. We were going out there to do a job, twist Hitler's tail, come back to a heroes' reception and get sloshed.

Our mission had been code-named 'Operation Chariton' for no reason other than that the name had no connection whatsoever with anything we were doing. The original plan was that on landing we would split into three separate groups.

Salvadori, Keany and I were to head for Milan, where we would join a band of partisans called the Green Flames. Hope and Millard were to aim for Cisterna to link up with Colonel Toselli (Codename Otello), a former officer with the crack Alpini Regiment, who commanded a division known by the enemy as 'The Bandits of Cisterna'.

This group of Partisans were so active, so effective and so feared by the occupying forces that the Germans were afraid to venture outdoors at night.

Our sixth man, Giovanni, was to leave us immediately after the landing to take part in an independent action with other American agents from the O.S.S.

For security reasons I knew nothing of Giovanni's plans. We worked on a 'need-to-know' basis, and as a radio operator with the Salvadori-Keany mission to Milan there was no point in my being informed of Giovanni's secret destination.

On the same principle I would have remained in ignorance of the Hope-Millard expedition to Cisterna if a tragic development had not led me to join them.

I found myself sitting opposite Giovanni on the floor of the spacious fuselage of the Dakota.

'Wounded already,' he said, grinning and indicating the cut above my left eyebrow. 'So what's the story?'

'You should see the other bloke,' I replied. (Original wit was not one of my strong points at that tender age.)

'That's right,' chipped in Busty. 'If that's what Bill does to his comrades, I shudder to think what he might do if he got hold of Adolf or Benito.'

Thus we were obliged to describe to our group the events of the previous evening. Five British members of the S.O.E. had gone out together for a night on the town in Celina, the airstrip village where we had arrived a couple of days earlier.

None of us knew when our various missions were going to start so we tended to live each night as if it might be our last. We were in a small bar and had sunk more than a few drinks when two negro G.I.s walked in. They ordered and kept to themselves at the other end of the bar.

Without warning and for no apparent reason, a sergeant in our group then said in a deliberately loud voice, 'I don't like drinking with niggers.' You could have heard a pin drop. A menacing silence fell on the company while staff and other customers waited to see what would happen next. To their credit, the two black soldiers quickly finished their drinks and walked away without a word. They avoided an unpleasant incident and to my way of thinking showed a great deal more dignity than the man who made the deliberately insulting and provocative remark.

I was furious with him. Black G.I.s had always been friendly and helpful towards me. Many were employed as truck and jeep drivers. They had often given me lifts along the highways and byways of Italy. Besides, they were on our side, for Heaven's sake! So I gave this sergeant a free and frank character assessment there and then in the bar. Our colleagues urged discretion and we avoided any violent scenes in public. But the resentment between us continued to ferment just below the surface. And when we reached the car park back at camp it boiled over into a full-blooded fight. Our comrades stayed out of it at first, but after several blows had been exchanged and we had rolled under a stationary truck, they pulled us apart before we could inflict any further damage on each other.

My rival's face was a mask of blood and I was bleeding from a cut on the forehead. As we were prised apart, the sergeant and I mouthed solemn threats about what we would do to each other next time we met. But that day has never dawned and I have never seen him since.

A few hours later, after a curtailed night's sleep, we were told Operation Chariton was being launched that night. I had been billeted in a house in Cecina with Busty and Giovanni. We received the briefest details of our flight plan from an S.O.E. captain. Then we had to check and recheck our equipment and prepare for our departure.

The story of my private battle the night before kept our team amused for a few minutes as we set off on our mission. The jokes and the idle chatter helped to keep our minds off the dangers which faced us.

Looking back, I wonder that I did not suffer from double incontinence at the thought of being parachuted behind enemy lines. Yet the light-hearted banter kept up our spirits and gave mutual support to our confidence.

Perhaps over the centuries men going into battle with a natural fear of pain and death have lifted each other's morale and courage in the same sort of way. It is interesting to speculate whether Alexander the Great, William the Conqueror, Ulysses Grant and Admiral Lord Nelson suffered the same agonies over whether their sphincter muscles would let them down at the crucial moment. I do not suggest Bill Pickering is in the same league as these mighty warriors of yesteryear, but they may well have undergone similar stomach-churning thoughts.

My own background was spectacularly ordinary. I was born on 21 September, 1923, in Oldham and named after my father, William Albert Pickering. Three years later my mother Florence had a daughter Marjorie, and that completed our family.

My paternal grandfather, Samuel Albert Pickering, had been the borough surveyor for Oldham and a leading member of the Freemasons. My father had been wounded by shrapnel from a shell burst at Messines while serving with the Loyal North Lancashire Regiment on the Somme. He carried the six-inch scar just below the shoulder blade to his grave in 1967, aged 70.

He had met my mother at the end of the war while she was working as a nurse at Boundary Park Hospital, Oldham. I think it must have been from my mother's side that I inherited my spirit of adventure − or folly.

Her father, Henry Lucas, had run away from a lucrative family farming business in the Sandbach area of Cheshire to join the circus. While his wife Beatrice was wondering what had become of her wayward husband, he was living with gipsies and learning to speak their Romany language. Eventually, other members of the family managed to trace the prodigal son and they bought Beatrice tickets for a show. It must have been quite a sight when she took her seat in the front stalls and recognized the immaculate circus

7

ringmaster with his waxed moustache as her missing hubby.

Suffice to say they were reunited and lived relatively happily ever after, although my maternal grandpa refused to settle for life as a farmer.

Whatever the reason, my mother grew up a passionate patriot. She always celebrated St George's Day on 23 April and the much-neglected Empire Day on 24 May in a way which few reserved Englishmen would dare to do for fear of embarrassment.

As a schoolgirl mother always took the part of 'Britannia' in the Empire Day play, and she was enormously proud of me when I was ultimately awarded the Military Medal for my Italian escapade.

But I am sure it was my mother, who died in 1981 aged 83, who moulded the mind of young Bill Pickering by teaching me songs on her knee like 'Rule Britannia,' 'What Is The Meaning of Empire Day?' and 'Soldiers Of The King.' My father, who had 'done his bit' in the Great War, was less obviously patriotic. He shared the cynicism of many old soldiers who had faced the horrors of real battle while fighting for their country.

Nevertheless I surrounded myself with books about British heroes like Wellington, Drake and Nelson. I immersed myself in more recent war history by reading avidly about Sebastopol, Gallipoli and the Somme.

While my dad worked as the manager of a small plumbing firm in Piccadilly, Manchester, I read about First World War flying aces such as McCudden, Ball and Bishop.

My first memories were the days when we lived above a small grocer's shop in Drury Lane, Hollinwood, run by my mum's parents. I grew used to the sound of marching feet at an early age.

At 6.30 am each weekday the lights would come on at the nearby mill and columns of women in clogs and shawls would start trooping to work along the cobbled streets. But my mother hated Oldham, and at the age of six I was uprooted from Hollinwood Junior School and transplanted in the middle-class atmosphere of the Old Moat Junior School, Withington, Manchester.

My parents had gone upmarket, moving to a three-bed-roomed garden terrace in Rippingham Road, Withington, and I was to thrive and prosper well at my new school. I passed my 11-plus exam and qualified for the Manchester Central High School. This enabled me to land a prestigious white-collar job as a junior accounts clerk at Burgons, the multiple grocers, where I was working when war broke out.

Herr Hitler's decision to invade Poland could not have come at a worse time for me. Two days earlier I had been showing off on a bicycle for the benefit of a young female cousin. She was slim, blonde and a juvenile version of Ginger Rogers in the looks department. I was approaching my 16th birthday. She was a year or two younger and at an impressionable age. But I doubt she was over-impressed with my cycling skills when a pedal hit the kerb and I was sent sprawling. My lower leg was broken just above the right ankle and I was encased in plaster. This was an especially unlucky break because I had been planning to join the Royal Engineers' cadets at All Saints, Manchester. By this time we could sense that war was brewing. When it came with me on crutches I cursed my bad luck, my own stupidity and my pretty cousin Mary.

It seems incredible now when I think back to those days, but I clearly remember praying that the war would not end before I had become fit enough to play my part in it. I had nightmares that it would be called off before I could get my leg out of plaster.

All around me young men were joining the Territorial Army. I was hopping mad in every sense of the phrase until November, 1939, when I could hobble sufficiently well to enlist in the Royal Engineers' cadet corps. A few months later the Dunkirk evacuations and Churchill's fighting speeches caused a further surge of patriotism within my tender young breast.

I signed up with the Local Defence Volunteers, a willing but ill-equipped body made up of those too young or too old to fight in the real British Army. The unflattering nickname for our initials was 'Look, Duck and Vanish'.

A few months later, with a Hitler invasion from Operation

Sealion feared at any moment, we were renamed the Home Guard, otherwise know as 'Dad's Army'. To some people it may have seemed a pathetic joke. To me it was deadly serious and boosted my determination to see some real action.

Although I was only 16 in the summer of 1940, I devised s simple plot which enabled me to join up a year earlier than the legal minimum of 18. I had been to the Navy Recruiting Office in Lloyd Street, off Albert Square, Manchester, on a reconnaissance mission. A four-mile round trip on a bicycle during my lunch break had shown me what I must do.

First I had to alter my birth certificate. This was the shortened form, printed on pink paper, which my parents used to keep with other important documents in a tin box in a dressing-table drawer in their bedroom. Sneaking up there and removing the certificate was an easy task.

Then, with the aid of some Sloanes ink eradicator, I was able to amend my date of birth from 1923 back to 1922 – ageing me 12 months at a stroke of the pen.

Unfortunately the longhand form of the date of registry was not so simple. Changing the written out year 'Nineteen hundred and twenty-three' to 'twenty-two' was no easy matter. I could think of no way to make the letters 'wo' fill the space vacated by the letters 'hree'.

In the end I decided to take a calculated risk. As this last troublesome word was on the bottom right-hand corner of the document, I bent it backwards and forwards repeatedly as if by constant carless handling. Eventually the offending corner and its giveaway letters 'hree' tore away and I had a passable document.

All that remained was for me to remove my national insurance card from the company safe at Burgons. I was worried in case it contained my genuine date of birth. I did not want to run the risk of my irate employers revealing to the army the fact that I was under age.

Perhaps I over-estimated my value to the firm, or perhaps they appreciated a young man's fighting, patriotic spirit. In any event Burgons made no trouble for me when they realized I had 'gone for a soldier'.

I had already planned my campaign to enlist by booking two days from my holiday entitlement on 23 and 24 September, 1940, just after my 17th birthday on the 21st of that month. On the 23rd I set off for work normally as far as my parents were concerned in suit, shirt and tie.

In fact I arrived a little earlier than usual at the office, removed my N.I. card from the safe and disappeared again before the manager came along to ask any awkward questions. As it turned out, my fears were unfounded because the card only revealed that I was 'under 21'.

So, armed with my self-forged birth certificate I set off for the Army Recruiting Office in Dover Street, Manchester, hoping that my baby face would not give the game away. But my document never attracted a second glance and I sailed through the medical examination to enlist in the Welch Regiment.

I went home that night at the usual time and tried to disguise my excitement at the prospects which lay ahead. To minimize the risks of exposure, I had not told a soul about my plans and it was agonizing that I had nobody with whom to share my feelings.

I was particularly upset that my scheme involved the deception of my family, but all was forgiven in the fullness of time. The following day I appeared to set off for work again as usual. In fact I collected a rail warrant from the Recruiting Office and was ordered to catch a train from London Road Station, Manchester, on the Wednesday morning to join my comrades at Pembroke Dock.

Before catching the train a mile from home I posted a letter to my parents in which I wrote: 'This is just to let you know I have decided to join the Army. I have been sent to Pembroke Dock and I will write to you when I get there.'

It was hardly the most poetic or sentimental of notes, but you must understand that by this stage I was trying to demonstrate that boyish affections had been replaced by manly determination.

By the time the staff at Burgons were wondering why junior clerk Pickering was so late for work, Private 3973906

Pickering was on his way to Pembroke to teach Adolf's boys a lesson.

Three other recruits were in the same compartment as we set off for South Wales. By an extraordinary coincidence George McCosh from Birkenhead, Harold Bailey from Sandbach, Fred Welsh from Holmes Chapel and I finished up in the same platoon together.

My first taste of army life at Pembroke was appalling — quite literally. The food was almost inedible. Mercifully there wasn't much of it or our cooks would have surely succeeded where the Axis powers failed. We quickly learned at the same time that when army officers ask routine questions about complaints, recruits are not actually expected to make any. Those who did were put on jankers to contemplate their folly.

Our quarters were little better than our food — a draughty exposed hut through which the wind whistled constantly both from the elements of nature and the flatulence of its occupants.

There was a marginal improvement two weeks later when our battalion was moved to Chepstow, but there we had to withstand the freezing perils of guard duty. One cold winter's night, standing as sentry overlooking an eerie wood, I could not resist the warmth of our hut stove. I abandoned my post and tried to thaw out by sneaking back to our quarters. Unfortunately the heat had a soporific effect upon me and I was discovered fast asleep by an orderly officer on his rounds. I had only been in the army for a couple of months and I was on my first disciplinary charge. Not the most auspicious of starts to a military career! The sentence for deserting my sentry post was two weeks in the camp nick.

My first leave was at Christmas, 1940, when I returned home by train to see the results of the German blitz of Manchester. I was surprised at the sense of determined and resolute normality in the behaviour of ordinary citizens who had seen entire streets and famous landmarks flattened.

There was a comical scene when I arrived and knocked on the door of the family home, which was now above a hairdresser's shop in Oxford Road, All Saints, near the Scala Cinema. As I knocked I was oblivious to the fact that the downstairs shop windows had been blown out in an air raid and I could have just stepped into the front room of the house without resorting to the door knocker.

It was an emotional reunion with my mum, dad and younger sister. My mum greeted me with a combination of relief and anger, hugs and scolds for the anxiety I had caused them. My father put on a show of reproval, but I felt I could detect a glint of manly pride in his eye. After all he had done the same and joined up under-age for the First World War 25 years earlier.

In January, 1941, our battalion was moved again to West Wretham, near Thetford in Norfolk, to prepare for the anticipated German invasion of the east coast. This was to be my home for the next fifteen months, guarding the aerodrome used by the 311 Czech Air Squadron.

From time to time we would fire Lewis guns at passing enemy aircraft as we played our small part in the Battle of Britain. To the best of my knowledge, on the rare occasions when the guns worked properly, none of us managed to hit anything or caused the Luftwaffe pilots a moment's concern.

We were doing 24 hours on duty followed by 24 hours off, sleeping in rat-infested pill-boxes while we guarded Britain's coastline. At one stage our entire platoon of thirty became lousy through washing in melted snow. We had to endure the indignity of being disinfested, which involved minute searches of our most intimate areas and haircuts which went from short-back-and-sides to the skinhead look.

As a growing boy I was still constantly hungry. I supplemented the army diet by fishing for carp and roach in small ponds near our camp. Coarse anglers will be horrified to learn that instead of throwing back my catch, I ate them with relish!

This unauthorized addition to rations gave me the energy to play soccer for the regiment in a series of three ding-dong battles against our Czech guests. I also competed in a cross-country race against our foreign allies, but when I went to support the Welch Regiment boxing team in Hornington,

Suffolk, I ended up in camp prison again. I explained to the officers that I had only intended to borrow the bicycle which had been left conveniently against a wall in the village. But it cost me a second spell of two weeks in the nick.

It was about this time that I successfully applied for a transfer from the Welch Regiment to the Royal Corps of Signals.

But the war was not going quite as I planned it. Apart from hopelessly long-distance pot-shots at Dornier and Heinkel bombers which passed overhead unscathed, I had been given no opportunity to cover myself in glory. I was among a great bunch of lads, barrow boys from Manchester and miners from Bolton and Accrington. And I knew they also served who only stood and waited. But I was itching to get the taste of battle, and it wasn't just the bodylice which were causing the itching.

My war so far had consisted of starving on army rations, freezing on guard duty, digging trenches round an aerodrome, being disinfested from vermin and spending four weeks in prison.

So when I saw a notice on the bulletin board asking for volunteers for commando and paratroop training I put my name down immediately. I figured that anything had to be an improvement on my present circumstances.

We were expected to exist on streaky bacon and watered-down beans after a plate of gooey porridge. I was sick of the sight of the boiled potatoes, swedes or cabbage which turned up every lunchtime, invariably followed by rice pudding containing three prunes to avoid constipation.

Such spending money as we received was squandered on dreadful sandwiches from the NAAFI made of beetroot, Bovril and Oxo just to keep up our strength. And if you stepped out of line, the M.P.s were as bad as any Nazis.

So when I heard nothing more about my offer to join the commandos or the paras I was feeling both depressed and frustrated. My luck changed when an officer assembled us all and asked for volunteers for especially dangerous duties.

It's a well known maxim amongst squaddies that you

never volunteer for anything. As a result I attracted more scorn then admiring glances when I was the only one in our platoon to raise my hand.

My name was noted and I heard no more. For several months I had been learning Morse code to train as a Signalman and I was transferred with several comrades to Catterick Camp in Yorkshire. There I became a B3 Radio Operator and on reaching a sending and receiving speed of 12 words per minute, my weekly pay was increased from 17s 6d. to the princely sum of 21s.

On my first leave I thumbed lifts on lorries back to Manchester, arriving home at teatime. An hour later a telegram arrived with the curt message: 'Return to unit. Posted.'

My excitement was mingled with annoyance that the news should interrupt my leave. So I decided to enjoy one night on the town before I hitch-hiked back to learn my fate. I had been selected for Parachute Training with the 1st Airborne Division at Chesterfield. Things were beginning to look up.

I do not know what facilities are provided for training the Paras of today, but I suspect they are given something rather better than the fuselage of a plane with a hole in it with which to practice their life or death techniques. We were told to keep our feet and knees tightly together as we jumped through this hole some 12 feet to the ground below. At the same time we were urged to tuck our elbows into our sides and the moment we touched down we let our legs buckle under us to produce a forward roll.

We practised over and over again to the point of tedium for two solid weeks, but at least I felt they were making a soldier out of me at last. All the trainees, from private to colonel, were under the jurisdiction of a training sergeant. He would discipline all ranks indiscriminately if they made any mistakes. I especially enjoyed the sight of one senior officer who had ignored an instruction. He was sent to the top of some scaffolding where he had to sit for half an hour repeating the words: 'I am a silly little boy.' This appealed to my left-wing political views of that time.

Most of all I enjoyed the improvement in the food. We were sent on tough assault courses, and as part of our fitness training we had to run everywhere 'at the double' outdoors. To compensate we were treated to steak and kidney pies with fresh vegetables at mealtimes.

The climax of our training were the real practice jumps from aircraft. Now I know there are some men who actually enjoy leaping out of planes into space. I can only say that I am not one of them.

Occasionally the 'chutes would not open and the expression for the way the victims died was to say they became 'Roman Candles'. This was a graphic description of what they looked like as they plummeted to earth. This thought was always with me at the last moment before I jumped.

It came back to me again as we flew towards Piedmont on that moonlit night in 1945. My first thought was the usual 'Is there any way I can get out of this without losing face?' When I realized there was no escape, I then made my usual promise to myself that I would never allow such a situation to arise again.

But then, as during training in 1942, I could see no digni-fied, let alone heroic, way back. In 1942 there were two things which kept me going. One was the absolute terror of being thought a coward by my comrades. The second was the target of a coveted red beret – sign of a fearless para-trooper and the passport to all the prettiest girls in town. So when I passed my parachute training and was awarded my new form of headgear to replace the uninspiring forage cap, I couldn't wait to test it out. We were sent to a mansion call-ed Fawley Court at Henley-on-Thames for further special-ized training. It was a magnificent building, set in its own grounds about a mile from the station. When I saw my new quarters for the first time, I decided that my war had taken a definite turn for the better.

But the army has a wonderful way of building you up so it can knock you down again. No sooner had I arrived and met my new bunch of forty or fifty signalmen than they confiscated our hard-earned red berets. I did not see the reasoning behind it at the time. I could only reflect ruefully that it was part of some heartless plot to prevent the female population of Henley falling head over heels in love with

Paratrooper Pickering. Only later did I learn that Fawley Court was one of the training bases used by the top-secret Special Operations Executive. Unknown to me, I had been accepted as a trainee with the S.O.E. and the wearing of red berets around the town would help to identify us as such to any Nazi spies or Fifth columnists.

When I started training at Henley in July, 1942, I had already mastered the art of sending and receiving Morse at a respectable 18 words per minute. It was now the task of four negroes from the General Post Office in Georgetown, British Guiana, to take our speeds up to 30 words a minute in five months. These men – Case, Lorimer, Lewis and Jackson – had enlisted in the army as training N.C.O.s and they could send messages at incredible speeds.

As wireless operators, building up our transmitting speeds was naturally the main priority, but we also had to go through a rigorous physical training schedule which involved learning the arts of ju-jitsu, unarmed combat, boxing and silent killing. Training hours were similar to those of school-children and at that age we still had enough energy to make the most of our free time in the evenings.

We adopted a local pub called the Old Bell Hotel as our regular home from home. Our army pay never went far enough for our thirsts, but I helped to supplement our incomes on the pub piano. I had a bit of an ear for music so I taught myself to pick out all the latest tunes. Although I would never have passed auditions for the Albert Hall, I was good enough to accompany the noisy G.I.s who crowded into the Old Bell for sing-songs. The Americans, who were drawing a fabulous £7 a week, were more than generous, if a little flashy, with their comparative wealth. From time to time they would lob a pound note on the piano and tell me and my mates, Jock Shannon and Bill Beggs, to get our-selves a drink. I blush to admit that we rarely remembered to give any change after we had visited the bar.

But one day all our penny-pinching at the Old Bell paled into insignificance when we struck it rich in a big way. On this occasion it was another Scotsman, Jock Reid, who found himself on the gravy train with Bill Beggs and myself. The three of us had managed to get into some sort of minor trouble with the authorities which resulted in our being put on fatigues. This consisted of cleaning corridors in the cellars of Fawley Court. We accumulated a pile of dust and couldn't be bothered to get rid of it properly. Instead we decided to lose it behind an old wooden door. That proved to be one of the best tactical decisions we could have made. Behind this ancient door was a maze of corridors which we explored. They led to an array of alcoves in which wine racks were stacked with bottles. It was an Aladdin's Cave for boozers. Claret, port and brandy had been laid down to improve with age. There were hundreds of bottles and we quickly came to the decision that they had matured for long enough. We liberated one bottle of old French Cognac and celebrated our good fortune in predictable style that night. Next day we formulated a plan to improve our finances. We synchronized our watches and crept out of bed at 2 am that night while the rest of our comrades slept. Our battledress was slipped on and we tip-toed down to the cellar again. This time we took twelve bottles of Cognac prisoner and evaded the sentries guarding the outside of Fawley House. This was easy because we were familiar, as insiders, with their routine. We crossed a large field and by the side of the main road to Henley we found a suitable ditch where we could hide our booty. After stowing our treasure, we crept back to our quarters, undressed, climbed quietly back into bed and slept the sleep of the innocent. The next evening, after dark, we returned to our hidden cache and removed one bottle. Billy Beggs and I then took it to a well known pub in Henley where we sought out the landlord for a quiet chat. We showed him our bottle of Cognac and asked if he would like to buy any. Instead of jumping at the prospect as we had anticipated, the landlord seemed over-cautious and asked all sorts of awkward questions. With hindsight I suppose he must have wondered whether he was being set up. Billy and I were getting nervous and we were starting to consider Plan B — running away as fast as our legs could carry us. But, just before we set off, he offered us £1 a bottle. They were probably worth many times more during the war, but we were

1 The author, Algiers, 1943.

2 (below left) Corporal Busty Millard: "an affable character who liked nothing better than a pub crawl with the boys." (p.4)

3 (below right) The author, Billy Beggs and Alan Irvine, North Africa, 1943.

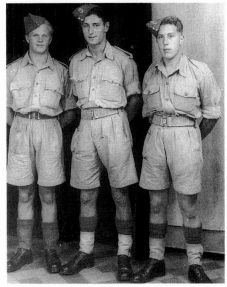

4 "Our first destination — a church at Mombarcaro." (p.24)

delighted to accept £12 for the dozen bottles, which seemed like a small fortune to us. We dashed back to where Jock was nonchalantly standing guard over the other eleven bottles. The deal was completed and we shared out the money. With £4 each in our pockets, we were wealthier than we had ever been in our lives.

Our behaviour was like little children on Christmas morning. We skipped and jumped for joy. Giggling like schoolgirls we ran to the posh Catherine Wheel Hotel in Henley where we ordered portions of hors d'oeuvres at 3s 6d each. This was unprecedented luxury at that time. The Catherine Wheel was full of officers and their lady friends, who looked askance at three common privates eating the finest food and drinking whiskies at an alarming rate. We neither knew nor cared what went through their minds, but it was a scene which was to be re-enacted many times in the course of the next few months.

Unhappily, all good things must come to an end, and in the autumn of 1942 we were given two weeks' embarkation leave prior to being sent abroad. We were issued with tropical kit, which convinced us that we were heading for somewhere cold. The army was perverse like that, assuming that careless talk would get back to enemy spies. So they would play tricks like issuing deceptive clothing to confuse them.

I returned to Manchester to see my family and to be wished a tearful bon voyage. When I caught the train back to Henley at the end of my leave, half of our group − some 25 wireless operators − had disappeared. Later I learned they had gone to the United States, where they were issued with American uniforms before joining in the invasion of North Africa. The rest of us had to wait a further three weeks before we took a different circuitous route to the same ultimate destination.

Our group caught a train to Gourock, Glasgow, where we boarded the S.S. *Arundel Castle* on the River Clyde. We had no idea where we were going. At that time we still didn't know that we were now members of an elite secret organisation called the S.O.E.!

There were to be several more adventures between

November, 1942, and February, 1945, but my thoughts were brought back to the present when our Piedmont-bound Dakota became the target of anti-aircraft guns as we crossed the coast of Genoa.

'It's only token stuff,' we were informed by our American pilot. 'Nothing to worry about.'

'Easier said than done,' I thought as we watched the tracer from the bullets flashing by.

The pilot was right. It was only slight flak which lasted less than a minute. But it was enough to concentrate our minds again on the tasks that lay ahead, and to remind us that we were now flying over enemy-held territory.

Ten minutes later we had reached our dropping zone and we started looking for the landing fires.

'There it is,' said the pilot.

'And there's another,' said I.

'And there's a third one,' said Salvadori.

The three landing fires — one genuine and two false lures — were to become symbolic of what we would be facing for the entire mission. One set had been lit by the Autonomous Partisans led by Major Enrico Mauri. Another had been ignited by the Germans as a decoy when they heard the aircraft engine and saw the first fire. The third, we later learned, had been started by the Italian Communists, who were hoping for a windfall of weapons which they thought we might be dropping to Major Mauri. Fortunately our pilot identified the correct pattern of fires after circling the area for twenty agonizing minutes. The red light came on and the six of us lined up. We were all wearing the Irvine Statachutes which opened automatically (or so we were assured!).

Hope, Keany, Giovanni, Millard and Salvadori went ahead of me at one-second intervals, giving me longer than them to reflect upon my stupidity for finding myself in such a situation. Then the despatching sergeant tapped me on the shoulder. I stepped out into space and felt the icy blast of the cold night air on my exposed face.

Before I had time to think further my 'chute had opened and I felt the welcoming tug of the harness on my shoulders. That slight pain produced a surge of relief as I realized I was not about to become a 'Roman Candle'.

As I floated down I had thirty long seconds to consider my situation. I was about to land 100 miles behind enemy lines, and the Germans had already lit a fire to welcome us. I looked upwards longingly at the disappearing Dakota.

II

INTO THE LIONS' DEN

My parachute training at Chesterfield had overlooked how to deal with snow landings. So after all those practice jumps in which I perfected my forward roll endless times, my touchdown in Piedmont scored no points for style, finesse or dignity. As I came down, my feet landed in the trailing parachute of Major Salvadori. He had completely disappeared and when I hit his billowing 'chute I slid forward as the snow gave way beneath it and landed flat on my back. The snow provided such a cushion that it was a happy landing for me. I unbuckled my harness and gathered in the parachute. Then I heard muffled moans beside me. It did not take a genius to work out that the desperate cries were coming from the Major. I could not make out exactly what he was saying but I gathered that he would prefer to be on top of the snow rather than underneath it. By using his 'chute as a starting point, I quickly dug my way towards him like a demented terrier sensing a rat. Within a few seconds I had reached Major Salvadori and cleared the snow from above his head.

'Thanks, Bill,' said the relieved Major. 'I owe you a pint.'

'First pub we find I'm going to hold you to that,' I replied.

As I was struggling to rescue Major Salvadori, the other members of our group were being rounded up by the Partisans and herded towards the nearby woods. Led by Major Enrico Mauri they collected the cylindrical tubes containing guns, ammunition and other supplies which had been dropped with us.

'Hurry up. The Germans are coming.' Although my Italian was limited I knew precisely what they were saying. I needed little encouragement to scamper towards the woods with my colleagues. Perhaps scamper is not quite the word to describe my attempt to hurry though six feet snow drifts. It was more of a combination of running and swimming.

As the last of us reached the cover of the woods, we looked back to see the first of the German troops cresting a hill half a mile away. They were just three silhouettes on the skyline, but the sight of them put the wind up me. I pointed them out to one of the Partisans, who laughed contemptuously at the approaching enemy.

'Do not worry my friend,' he explained. 'They have to *try* to find us. But they always come just too late. They are more afraid of catching up with us than we are of being caught. The Germans may occupy our country in the day-time, but we are in charge around here at night. If they get cheeky and come too close we will only have to fire one volley and they will scatter like chickens.'

Major Salvadori, whose Italian was fluent, later explained that the Germans could not be seen to ignore a blatant air-drop. Urged on by their deskbound commanders, the troops would be despatched on a seek and capture or destroy mis-sion. But they had little enthusiasm for the task with Major Mauri and his men around. The ordinary German soldiers trod carefully and timed their arrival impeccably to coincide with the departure of the Partisans.

So it was on this occasion where the Germans were just too late to get involved in any exchanges of gunfire. We even had time to collect the supply and ammunition canisters as well as our parachutes, which were later converted into silk pyjamas!

As we headed through the woods, there was a tremendous feeling of relief that the first part of our mission had passed off so successfully. Our confidence was also boosted by the fearless behaviour of the Partisans who were leading us to safety.

'Won't they try to follow us?' I had asked nervously.

'Of course not,' said one of my Italian comrades.

'Why not?' I asked in sincere ignorance.

'In case they find us,' he replied, slapped me on the back and roared with laughter.

Such confidence was contagious. I started laughing too. In my newly-found false sense of security, I actually started to believe my worries were over.

Meanwhile a terrible argument had broken out between Captain Keany and a Partisan named Giacomo Bagnasco. Here we were, in enemy-held territory crawling with Germans, when these two decided to have a fierce row about — cigarettes! Giacomo was a huge fellow with a booming voice. Although he was only 18, he was already a giant of a man. How typical of Captain Keany that this should be the comrade with whom he should pick a quarrel. The gist of it was that one of the supply canisters had contained several cartons of Gold Flake cigarettes for the exclusive use of the dropping party. Keany, who had a reasonable command of Italian, had overheard the Partisans discussing this 'windfall'. Giacomo, who had a distinctive voice full of local dialect expressions, was accused of directing the operation to plunder our cigarette supply. Keany interrupted our escape from the approaching Germans to accuse our new allies of being thieves and liars. Our Irish friend certainly had a rare sense of diplomacy, priorities and timing. Fortunately Major Salvadori intervened and told the irate Captain to calm down and to concentrate on the job in hand. For a moment I had thought that Keany and Bagnasco were going to come to blows in what would have been a memorable fight.

But tempers cooled and we continued our journey through the tall coniferous trees which provided our cover. From what I observed later, it seemed that Captain Keany's blood got up whenever he spotted the enemy. Tactical decisions not to engage in a pitched battle left him seething with frustration, and he had to blow his top with somebody.

After a 30-minute march through the woods, our party reached our first destination — a church at Mombarcaro. As we emerged from the darkness into the moonlit clearing, I took my first relaxed opportunity to study closely the Partisans and their leader. They were an unlikely looking bunch and I remembered Wellington's remark some 140 years earlier. On seeing his ragamuffin troops in the Peninsular Campaign, he had declared 'I don't know what effect these men will have upon the enemy, but, by God, they terrify me.'

In their odd assortment of uniforms, Major Mauri's men looked equally menacing. Some wore old Italian army jackets; others wore Nazi trousers. Some combined both. They might have been to an end-of-war jumble sale. With their baggy trousers, long boots and ammunition belts, plus an assortment of machine guns, rifles and pistols, they gave the appearance of a chorus of brigands from some Gilbert and Sullivan opera.

Their main distinguishing feature was their blue neckerchiefs, tied rakishly at the front with a large knot at the throat, but falling to a point at the back of their necks like overgrown Boy Scouts. Yet their disorderly outfits were in contrast to their total obedience and eager discipline whenever Major Mauri issued instructions. He was a tall, slim, elegant man, wearing a light jacket with a sub-machine gun hanging casually over his right shoulder. Apart from his more respectable appearance, the Major's polite but assertive manner singled him out from his men, who obviously adored him. Major Mauri directed operations at the church along with Captain Hugh Ballard, the S.O.E. agent who had been waiting to meet us at the dropping ground.

The Captain was a South African of medium height but thick-set build. He also had what seemed to be a regulation moustache in this part of the world. It grew the same colour as his mousey hair. Captain Ballard wore a long woollen jumper which hung over his trousers. If you had swapped his sub-machine gun for a 12-bore shotgun, you could have sworn the captain was out for a spot of grouse-shooting on the Glorious Twelfth.

The church, which stood in splendid isolation in a clearing, was a small, whitewashed, one-storey affair with a cross over the front door. Mauri and Ballard supervised the Partisans as they carried the guns, ammunition and supplies into the church, where, I later learned, they were hidden in the cellars.

At this point Keany and I were allocated an Italian guide to take us towards Brusasco. Our limited Italian meant we had to head for Milan in a more roundabout way than Major Max Salvadori, who spoke the language like the native he was.

Keany and I shook hands with Major Max just outside the church, as we were the first to leave.

'See you in Milan,' shouted Keany as we turned to depart. It was a typically cheerful and positive remark from my Irish pal. Unhappily it was a promise which was not fulfilled.

Our guide led us on a two-hour walk from the church. We travelled in Indian file with the Partisan leading and Keany following him. I brought up the rear. To amuse myself I tried to think of a funny story about the Italian, the Irishman and the Englishman tramping through snow by moonlight behind enemy lines, but none came to mind.

From time to time we would come close to an isolated farmhouse and dogs would start barking. The first time it happened I flung myself head first into a snowdrift, terrified in case the dogs brought a couple of Panzer divisions down upon us. But my ungallant and undignified behaviour only brought mocking laughter from our Italian escort and the devil-may-care Keany. The guide assured me once more that we had nothing to fear from the Germans at night. I was never wholly convinced.

For the journey I was carrying my wireless transmitter, the Partisan toted the cumbersome generator and Keany humped the batteries along with him. Wireless operators are not especially popular in this situation, but we do come in handy when assistance is needed.

It was just before dawn at around 5 am when we arrived at a farmhouse some 300 yards north of the large village of Monesiglio. It was the home of anti-Fascist sympathizer 'Tal' Biestro and his wife Luisa. We hid out of sight while our guide knocked on the door and checked that the coast was clear. To my horror, he had explained en route that the village was occupied by dozens of German and Italian Fascist troops. They used it as a base from which to carry out their *rastrellamenti*. This alarming word, which sounded to me like some hideous form of torture from the days of the Spanish Inquisition, in fact means 'raking out'. These operations were being carried out constantly throughout this area of the province, usually by the despised S.S. Their quarry was the Partisans and S.O.E. agents like Keany and myself. I was not anticipating a good night's sleep with them 300 yards down the road. But we were given a warm welcome by the Biestros, who tried to explain to me: 'The Germans would never think of looking so close. They would never believe you would dare to hide so near them. They are very efficient and logical. We use that against them. Their efficiency and logic will lead them away from here. The last place the Fascists will look is under their own noses. They will think you would have to be mad to stay here at the edge of Monesiglio.'

I am sure Tal, Luisa and our guide were trying to reassure me, but I found little source for comfort in their encouraging words. I had volunteered three years earlier for dangerous duties, not for suicide missions with crackpot Italians and a mad Irishman. But I was well and truly stuck with it now. Up a certain smelly creek without a paddle.

If I sound ungrateful, it is only because I did not share the amazing courage of this ordinary working class couple, who were risking their lives to shelter us. They were poor farmers who barely scratched a living on the handful of acres of hilly land where they grew maize and raised chickens.

Tal was a red-headed man. Although of medium size, he dwarfed his petite dark-haired wife. They made it clear that although they had precious little for themselves, they were eager to share it with us. So we had our first meal of Operation Chariton in the farmhouse kitchen of the Biestros. We sat round a wooden table on wooden chairs which rested on a stone-flagged floor. Around the fireplace was an impressive array of earthenware pots and fire-blackened pans. An old-fashioned cooking pot hung over the fire like some sketch from a Dickensian novel.

Our meal of stewed steak and coarse bread was as good

as any feast after that long march. The red wine helped to wash it down and soon I was feeling better again. The second course was a dish called polenta — a yellow porridge-type substance made from maize and milk with which I was to become all too familiar in the weeks ahead.

Our hosts had obviously helped the Autonomous Partisans before. They knew better than to ask questions about the nature of our mission or where we were heading next. Instead, they asked in helpfully slow Italian, 'Did you have a pleasant flight?' And, 'Was it a nice walk?'

Their questions gave the proceedings an air of unreality. Keany could not have been happier. Having dropped into the lion's den, we had crept right up to the lion without being spotted. Keany thought this was a great lark.

Minutes before dawn our new hosts led us to a hut which was to be our home from home for the next three weeks. To reach it we had to walk steeply uphill for 200 yards. It was a stone building some 7 feet square with a roof about 10 feet high in the middle.

The Biestros may have tried to explain what normal function it served, but I could not understand them. As far as I could see it did nothing except store dried leaves. Whether they could be used as fuel I never did find out. All I know is that a bed of leaves is as comfortable as any bed of goosedown when you are as worn out as we were by this time. Our landlord and landlady promised to warn us if any Germans approached from the village. They showed us how easily we could burrow under the 4 feet pile of leaves to hide.

As I drifted off to sleep I was thinking about how easy it would be to find somebody under the leaves with a rifle and bayonet. Nevertheless I slept like a baby throughout the rest of the morning and part of the afternoon. When the first stirrings of consciousness returned to my sleepy head, I took a few seconds to recollect my bearings. But soon enough I remembered. I was a hundred miles behind enemy lines and in a tiny hut 500 yards from a German garrison. Immediately I was wide awake.

Keany was aroused from his slumbers at the same time and we both eased ourselves out of our leafy mattress to study our situation. The snow was still lying thick around us and coating the roofs of the village of Monesiglio. Through the binoculars we could now see our enemy going about their business.

German soldiers wandered down the main street in their grey uniforms and distinctive helmets. Some patrols were on ordinary bicycles. Others were on motor-bikes and in jeeps or trucks. It was certainly a hive of activity which we observed with caution from a vantage point near our hut.

The village had a main square, two or three bars-cum-cafés, a church, a school and a few shops. The troops seemed to be billeted in the local school. Darkness fell as we studied our new environment.

'Well Bill,' grinned Keany 'I think we're going to like it here.'

By arrangement, we waited until 6 pm before making our way carefully to the farmhouse. We crept up to the building, checked that all was well and knocked on the door. The Biestros ushered us in for supper and made us welcome once more.

They answered all our questions about Monesiglio and advised us that virtually all the villagers loathed the presence of Hitler's occupying forces. It was becoming increasingly obvious that the Führer was losing the war and the Italian people wanted an end to the fighting and to Fascism.

But the Biestros warned that some of the local villagers had sons or husbands still fighting with the Italian Republican Army led by Mussolini. They may have lost their appetite for the continuing losing struggle, but they were still loyal to their commanders and followed their orders. So the surrounding population, although overwhelmingly pro-Partisan, might include one or two Nazi informants. It was an unnerving thought for the next few weeks. All the people we ultimately met from Monesiglio could not do enough to help us. Yet there was always the constant nagging doubt that some collaborator might give the game away.

After a tasty supper of farmhouse food and an informal briefing about the village, Keany and I retired to our quarters for what was to be our regular 11 pm broadcast back to London. From my quartz crystal transmitter, I reported that our party had landed safely.

I was using a 'one-time pad' to disguise my report. This had its only counterpart back in S.O.E. headquarters in Baker Street where they could unscramble my cryptic messages, sent in Morse code. Then it was my turn to take down H.Q.'s messages for the Operation Chariton team.

After the first night's jottings had been transmitted and received, Keany and I knew we were immediately at the top of the wanted list for the Germans in Monesiglio. They would have picked up our signals and realized from the wavelength that they were coded messages being sent to and from England. Although this was an uncomfortable consideration, we had been assured during our pre-mission briefing that, provided we kept our broadcasts under an hour in length, we would remain undetected. The Germans had radio direction finding vehicles which they would mobilise as soon as we started transmission, but they needed an hour to set up two separate 'fixes' on our position.

Keany always kept a vigilant look-out, sub-machine gun at the ready, while I was working. But I didn't need any encouragement to limit the transmissions to less than an hour. Just to make things a little more confusing for Jerry, we also moved occasionally to different venues for our 11 o'clock radio programme.

As the days went by, Partisans would meet us at the Biestro farmhouse to deliver and receive messages. One of them brought with him our two parachutes from their hiding place at the church of Mombarcaro. Under cover of darkness he led us to the village tailoress in Monesiglio, a trusted sympathizer.

When our guide introduced us as two British agents, she embraced Keany and I warmly, oblivious or uncaring that German soldiers were sleeping in the same village a few yards away.

'It is wonderful to have you here,' said this tall, slim lady whose brown hair was tied up in a schoolmarm-style bun. 'The sooner your friends come and kick these German swine back to Berlin, the better it will be for everybody.'

The tailoress took our measurements and judged that she would be able to make us a dressing gown and two pairs of pyjamas each out of the silk material. I reckoned that would leave her a few yards extra to make several pairs of green, brown and black knickers for the ladies of the village as well. But we did not care as long as they did not 'fall into German hands' in any sense of the phrase. Keany had a long, animated conversation with the tailoress to that effect. She smiled at his suggestion, but then put on a reproving face and said: 'None of my friends would dream of fraternizing with the Boche.'

As we left our seamstress by her back door, we explained that we did not know when we would be coming back to collect the garments.

'We'll see you in a few weeks when the war is over,' said the ever-confident Keany.

Our visit to the tailoress was one of our more frivolous trips to Monesiglio at night, but we did have to go there on business from time to time to recharge my radio batteries. It had not taken Keany and I long to realize that the hand generator was far too time-consuming for everyday use. As an emergency stand-by it had its uses, but it would take a team of men working at half-hour intervals the best part of a day to fully charge the batteries. When Keany and I tried it on our own, we were running our own strength down as fast as the batteries were charging up. Taking it in turns, and occasionally using our feet to rotate the winding mechanism, we exhausted ourselves just to gain a few minutes transmission time. So we were mightily relieved when a Partisan heard of our plight and took us into Monesiglio to meet another anti-Fascist sympathizer with his own electrical workshop. We would take the batteries in around midnight after our regular transmission was over and leave them with him. The following evening they would be brought by Partisan courier to the farmhouse for our collection, all charged up again and ready for action. They would then last for three days.

These necessary trips into Monesiglio, which passed without incident, emboldened Keany to the point where he ordered me to accompany him one night for a drinking session. Do not misunderstand me. I have never needed any encouragement, let alone an order, to go for a drink. But even by Keany's laid-back standards, this seemed a little reckless.

We had watched the Germans that day leaving the village by foot, bicycle, motor-cycle, sidecar, jeep and truck. Our own spy network soon told us they were going miles away to hunt for the new British broadcasting team, i.e. us.

This piece of intelligence delighted Keany. The thought of the Germans scouring the area but overlooking their own backyard appealed to his mischievous sense of humour. And so it was that night I found myself in a bar in the heart of a German garrison, drinking several bottles of red wine.

'Isn't this delightful?' beamed Keany to me, as our Partisan pals kept watch for the returning soldiers.

I had been full of apprehension as we took our usual cautious route through the farmyards and back streets to the centre of the village. But the assurances we had received that the Germans were all out searching for us proved to be true. And after the first two nervous glasses, I started to wind down and enter the spirit of Keany's great joke. Fortunately I stayed just sober enough to resist the temptation to sing 'Rule Britannia' and to talk Keany out of performing his moving rendition of 'Danny Boy'.

Our foolhardy night on the town was happily uneventful. As Keany and I zig-zagged our way back to our little stone hut, each making even louder shushing noises between bouts of giggling, we must have looked like a pair of music hall drunks. But we lived to fight another day, and the next day was almost a disaster for us.

After recovering from our king-sized hangovers we decided it was time to move away from the hut again for our night-time broadcast. It was a sensible precaution which nearly cost us our lives. We were walking up a woodland path towards a small hill which overlooked the immediate area. As we sauntered along, brimming with confidence after our recent escapade, Keany decided to take a leak. It seemed like a good idea, so I joined him. From force of habit we both walked a few feet away from the trail and stood behind a convenient bush. No sooner had we started to empty our bladders than a German foot patrol rounded the bend. I have never felt so vulnerable. Potty-training as a toddler is obviously a salutary lesson and my first thought, strangely enough, was to avoid wetting my pants. On the other hand, when man has allowed nature to start its course, there is a problem in turning off the supply.

In our confusion, Keany and I stood statue-still behind the bush with our fully-loaded 'weapons' held tightly in our hands to stem the flow while our guns were slung over our backs. We dared not breathe as a dozen Nazis marched past us three yards away.

What they would have made of the sight if they had glanced in our direction, Heaven knows. If they had ordered us to put up our hands they might have got a soaking. But our ploy worked and the Germans never spotted us. Perhaps I could add a chapter to the S.O.E. manual entitled 'What to do if the enemy approaches while you are urinating.'

It was a tremendous relief, in more ways than one, when the chattering Nazis finally disappeared from view and earshot. Keany and I vowed that we would take our leaks in turns in future while the other stood guard.

There was another occasion a few days later when our search for another transmitting spot nearly led us into an enemy platoon. They were obviously in the area looking for us and fortunately we saw them first. Keany and I crept behind a hedgerow and crawled at record-breaking speed into the undergrowth. We made our way cautiously but speedily to the nearest farmhouse. When the occupants saw us in our British battledress, they were horrified. The women started weeping and wailing, begging us to leave them alone. We explained that we meant them no harm and that we were hiding from a German patrol which was approaching.

'German soldiers come with guns,' said Keany in his basic Italian. 'We British. We hide from them.'

That little speech only made things worse. The sobbing

increased in volume. The farmer's wife explained, 'If the Germans find you here they may kill us or burn down our farm.'

I was too scared to argue. 'If the Germans find us they will certainly kill us. So shut up and go away,' I told them abruptly, at the same time taking the safety catch off my Marlin.

That seemed to do the trick. Without another word, the farmer's wife and family scampered indoors, leaving Keany and I peeping over the farmyard wall behind our sub-machine guns.

There was nowhere for us to hide because there was a steep uphill climb behind the farm where we would have been easy targets. So we crouched and waited, knowing that if the platoon came towards us we would have to take out every one of them before they could pin us down and call up reinforcements. Mercifully, the Nazis headed in a different direction and we never saw them again that day. It is a chilling thought that if those Germans had turned left instead of right, the next 40 years of my life would probably never have happened.

That night we received instructions to meet another S.O.E. agent who was being parachuted into the Mombarcaro area. He was a captain who used the *nome di battaglia* of 'Roccia' (pronounced Rosher). Our instructions were to make our way to the dropping zone and prepare a sequence of fires. When we saw the Dakota fly over, it would signal two letters to me in Morse. I was to reply from the ground with another two letters flashed by torch. Then eight fires were to be lit in the shape of a 'T' to signal it was all clear for Roccia to jump. Another canister of supplies was dropped at the same time containing more arms, ammunition and assorted goodies.

Roccia was being flown in to support Major Hope and Corporal Millard who were having trouble with the lingo. It seemed the Major was experiencing great difficulty making himself understood by the Partisans because of his clipped colonial accent.

Our H.Q. staff wanted to step up the guerrilla warfare

which the Italian resistance forces were waging on the increasingly demoralized occupation powers.

Under his real name of Luigi Cavalieri, Roccia had been a lawyer in Rome before the war. His wife and child still lived there, which was why he used a 'battle name' alias. He was a short, stocky individual in his mid-forties, balding and with the almost obligatory moustache.

The local Partisans joined Hope, Millard, Keany and myself as a reception committee for his arrival. Although Roccia was an excitable character whose heart sometimes ruled his head, he was obviously popular with his Italian comrades, who gave him a warm welcome.

We quickly led him through the woods to the clearing at Mombarcaro where the church stood. Keany made sure our cigarette supply arrived unscathed on this occasion. We stuffed as many cartons as we could manage into our pockets before giving a parting farewell to our mates. Then we went our separate ways, with Keany and I looking decidedly fatter than when we arrived as our clothing bulged with packets of Gold Flake.

As Hope, Millard and Roccia supervised the storage of supplies at the church, Keany and I set off back towards our little stone hut.

'We may run out of food or ammo,' said Keany, 'but I reckon we've enough fags to see the war out.'

III

IMMINENT DANGER

Much of our time in Monesiglio was uneventful and many of the days have blurred together with the passage of time. Sending military messages back home from enemy-occupied territory became a matter of mundane routine, hard though that may seem to believe. But every now and again we would receive a severe jolt to shake off any thoughts of complacency.

Such was the case one day when we set off for a long march from our hut to relay and receive our daily reports. I well remember it was a warm, dry morning causing a mist to rise from the cold ground as the sun gradually illuminated the hillside.

Familiarity breeds contempt, they say, and we had become rather blasé about the area above the village. Over the course of a few days we got to know every twist and turn of the trail, every rock and every tree en route. There had never been any sign of life, not even a goatherd or a shepherd to create a momentary sense of danger. So with this false sense of security wrapped around us like a cloak, we chatted unconcernedly as we headed for the hills.

'I think a picnic is called for,' said Keany. 'Look what I've got for us.'

My Irish friend then produced a cream cloth containing half a dozen raw eggs. It seemed he had 'liberated' them from a farm near our hideout just before dawn. I contributed my two chunky loaves provided by the Biestros and a large portion of salami sausage which I had scrounged from one of the Partisans in exchange for a few cigarettes.

'What a feast,' observed Keany, who proceeded to give me a pathetic example of an Irish jig while singing some Gaelic lament hideously out of tune.

In fact Keany, it transpired, was very much an Anglicised Irishman. He told me he had worked in some British civil service-type job before war broke out. While his Irish government 'dragged their feet', as Keany put it, he wasted no time in joining up with the British Army.

'You don't really deserve me,' he joked, 'but any enemy of Hitler is a friend of mine.'

As we walked I had told him of my early days in Oldham and how my patriotic fervour had caused me to forge my birth certificate so I could enlist. We both laughed when I explained: 'I was afraid it would all be over before the first Christmas.'

I told Keany about my training with the S.O.E. and how I had arrived in northern Italy via North Africa, Sicily and Anzio. We swapped many a tale and found we had shared similar experiences without ever meeting.

Eventually, in a distant valley, we reached a perfect spot for our picnic. It was just below a ridge which overhung a group of rocks. By pressing ourselves against them we were out of sight of anybody who looked down from the ridge above. By now there was a gentle breeze and that would carry the sound of our voices away in the direction of Monesiglio, which was now well out of sight.

We enjoyed our lazy luxurious lunch, accompanied by copious quantities of red wine. Then it was time for me to send a routine message back to our base in southern Italy, from where it could be relayed to our headquarters in Baker Street, London.

I was half way through my uninspiring report of troop movements when the silence of that early spring day was shattered by a series of explosions. Instinctively, Keany and I flung ourselves on to the ground when we heard the sounds of battle. At first we assumed that we were the targets for all this sudden attention. But as the seconds passed, we realized the firing was taking place on the ridge above and was not directed at us. I had time to send the coded message 'I am in imminent danger' before breaking off contact.

Then Keany motioned for me to follow him as he probed for a route which would take us to the top of the ridge. He was indicating by sign language not because he was afraid of being overheard, but because the row above us was so intense that we could not hear each other above the din.

Eventually Keany found a scarcely-used sheep track along the rock face. We clambered and scrambled along it until we reached the lip of the ridge. And there we saw a truly memorable sight. The landscape ahead of us dipped slowly down to a winding road, not normally used by military traffic. But a German convoy had obviously decided to take this unusual route to avoid any Partisan ambush. I have to tell you that the German plan had gone spectacularly wrong.

The Partisans had a remarkable intelligence network which provided information about enemy troop movements. On this occasion Keany and I soon worked out what had happened. Three troop-carrying lorries, flanked on either side, by two motor-cyclists led and followed by armoured trucks carrying mounted machine guns, had been waylaid by a band of Garibaldinis. These were the Communists who sported red neckerchiefs to identify their political persuasions.

As we adjusted to the deafening noise and the billowing smoke of battle, it became like an elongated three-dimensional scene from a movie — and we were sitting in the front row!

One of the German motorcycles was lying on its side on the grass at the side of the road. The body of the rider was lying nearby, his helmet blown in half and his face a grotesque mask of blood. One of his legs was missing and it looked as though he had hit a mine.

Another motor-cyclist was racing away from the column, presumably to fetch assistance, but he got only 50 yards from the rear of the convoy when we saw his machine slew sideways and the rider catapult through the air. Bullets riddled his body as it skidded along the roadway.

One of the German trucks had pulled off the left side of

the road and an heroic machine-gunner was pouring bullets towards the natural trench where the ambushers lay. He kept their heads down long enough for some of his comrades to leap out of the three trucks which had stopped in their tracks on the road.

It was obvious that some of the German soldiers had been picked off as soon as they jumped down. Half-a-dozen bodies lay at the foot of each lorry. On one of them a soldier was dangling from the tailgate with his arm pointing downwards and his head facing skyward with a puzzled expression on his face. The other truck was unoccupied apart from a figure in the driver's seat slumped over the wheel. His colleagues had tried to reach the machine gun from what we could guess, but three had already failed. A fourth had actually reached the gun and his still bleeding body was now draped across it.

At first it was hard to judge how many Garibaldini were taking part in the ambush. They were well hidden, unlike the German infantrymen who could find no cover by the roadside and who were well and truly pinned down.

As the Nazis fired at the Italian Communists on our side of the road, they were met by a fresh threat from the opposite side. Another band of Garibaldini on the far side, who had been holding their fire until this moment, suddenly opened up with a deadly fusillade. Many of the German soldiers never knew what had hit them. As they lay or knelt on the road facing us, they were hit from the rear. Some were flung forwards by the impact as one by one they were systematically wiped out. The exception was the machine-gunner on the lead vehicle. He was enjoying a charmed life, and some of his comrades managed to dash across to help him. They took a fearful toll in dead and injured as the Garibaldini on the far side of the road picked them off. But the Germans could see that reaching the truck could be their only hope of salvation. One of the now empty lorries was in the line of fire to the armoured truck, sheltering it from the sharp-shooters on the far side.

From our grandstand view we could see that the Partisans on our side were having more than enough trouble staying alive as the courageous German, now aided by two comrades, continued to rake them with fire. Those guns are not lightweight and his arms must have ached as he swung back and forth for what seemed like an eternity.

Keany and I saw a group of Garibaldini scurrying along behind him, trying to get to the other side of the sheltering lorry. By this time all three lorries appeared to be empty and their former occupants were scattered along the roadway, dead or dying. Only four Germans were now left to fight, and it seemed they were about to breathe their last. Yet fortune favours the brave in battle and the dark-haired, slightly-built machine-gunner must have felt the draught of some bullets whistling past his ears from the Partisans behind him. He spun round with the gun and caught three of them with his first burst. One of his colleagues had managed to get the truck started and another was feeding the magazine. The fourth survivor had been taken out by the surprise attack from the rear.

Despite my loyalties for the allied cause and my hatred of the enemy, a tiny part of me wanted those three remaining soldiers to escape. But it was not to be.

Just as the truck started to pick up speed, its occupants were caught by a withering hail of fire from the Garibaldini on our side of the road. They had taken advantage of the respite when the machine gun swivelled. After peeping over their trench and seeing their opportunity, a dozen of them had let the Germans have it with everything they had. The truck careered off the road, struck a rock and flipped on to its side. Another burst from the Partisans made certain of their fates. I felt strangely sorry, somehow, that the German who had caused so much trouble was just as dead as the rest of them.

The din of battle had been so great that the silence which followed was almost as frightening. Some seventy Germans had been killed in the attack and now we were able to count the numbers of their opponents as they slowly emerged from cover. There were about twenty on our side of the road and a dozen on the other. They had lost five men dead and a further nine wounded. And boy, were they pleased with themselves!

They took off their hats and waved and cheered at each other across the roadway. I turned to Keany and asked, 'What do we do now, sir?'

'Absolutely nothing,' whispered Keany. 'We'll wait for the buggers to clear off and then we'll scarper ourselves. That glorious escapade will bring Adolf's boys pouring into the area. We could have done without it. But what a lovely show they put on for us.'

We watched in silence as the Partisan force, heavily laden with captured weapons, began to melt into the far hillside. Then we carefully crawled back from our ridge and down to the site of our picnic. Keany scoured the area for signs of our presence, like crumbs and cigarette ends.

Satisfied we had left no trace of our existence, he led us back in the general direction of Monesiglio. We took a slightly different route, keeping away from the beaten track in case we blundered into any Germans who might have been rushing to the area. As we walked, Keany told me in a low voice that he did not entirely trust the Garibaldini section of the Partisans.

'The anti-Fascist war is coming to an end, and we'll probably be fighting those Commies next,' he explained. 'They know it. We know it. They know we know it. We know they know we know it. That's why I didn't stop to say hello.'

Keany was more aware of the political implications of the situation than I. There were no less than six different types of Partisan. We worked mainly with the Autonomous group, distinguished by their blue neckerchiefs. They were a non-political band who hated Mussolini and the Fascists.

The Garibaldini were Communists who wore red neckerchiefs and divided their time between ambushing Fascists and preparing for the revolution against capitalism. The Justice and Liberty group were Liberals; the Action Party were Social Democrats; the Matteotti Socialists were a left wing Labour group who stopped short of Communism; and the Christian Democrats eventually led the country back to normality after the war.

Different groups would all work together for the common good on occasions, and in the S.O.E. we were supposed to encourage cooperation. But in reality we shared the general distrust of the Garibaldini, knowing this month's allies could be next month's enemies.

Having broken off my radio transmission at the start of the ambush, I knew I must wait 24 hours before I could contact our base at Monopoli, near Bari, again. For a day the Fannies (First Aid Nursing Yeomanry) and fellow Signalmen at base would have to wonder what had become of Sergeant Pickering.

They would have to decide whether to relay the message to the Baker Street headquarters of S.O.E. in London that I had sent them a QUG signal. This was part of the 'Q Code' – a shorthand form of Morse. The letters QTC told the receiver: 'I have a message for you.' QSA and a number from 1 – 5 told them the strength of their signal, with 5 the clearest and 1 the faintest. QRK? asked: 'What strength are you receiving me?' And QUG meant: 'I am breaking off transmission because I am in imminent danger.'

That was the last message I sent to Monopoli before the Garibaldini ambush on the Germans. Now our first priority was to leave the area of the attack without being detected. We decided to put as much distance as possible between us and the ill-fated convoy without rushing into the arms of any enemy patrols who would be heading for the battle zone. Our aim was to find a suitable hiding place where we could lie low until darkness fell. We had two dangerous roads to cross and we had no intention of doing so in broad daylight.

During our S.O.E. training, which we shared with the S.A.S., the S.B.S., Royal Marine and Royal Navy commandos, Keany and I had been taught how to build a comfortable 'nest' when sleeping in the open air. We would find a nice big bush and then lay a mattress of twigs below it. We would use our bodies to flatten any sharp points. Then, with this three-inch cushion keeping our bodies off the frozen ground, we would huddle together.

This training was perfected when we were dumped 100 miles from our base in the wild countryside of southern Italy with one shilling and a bar of chocolate in our pockets. We were told to use our initiative to live off the land as we made our way back to our training camp. In theory we were expected to find eggs, edible mushrooms and wild berries to sustain us on the picturesque mountainsides. In reality we had a tendency to behave like brigands and highwaymen, hijacking every form of transport from mule to steam train. But at least it taught us how to snatch sleep whenever it was available, regardless of whether we were tired. So by mid-afternoon Keany and I were slumbering peacefully beneath a bush, oblivious to whatever searches the Germans may have been making for the band who had attacked and killed their colleagues.

It was nearly 10 pm and clouds were veiling the moonlight when we awoke simultaneously as usual and set off to return to the comparative safety of our stone hut. We scattered our mattress of twigs, ate the rest of our bread and salami, almost emptied our wine flasks and ventured forth in the darkness. Using the stars as direction finders, we soon came across the track which would eventually lead us to Monesiglio. Once again our confidence improved with nightfall and we had no great fears of meeting enemy patrols en route. But we took extra precautions when we crossed the two roads which linked hillside villages in the valleys. Keany chose a crossing point on a sharp bend where there was limited vision in either direction. Then we split up and checked for 100 yards each way to make sure nobody was lying in wait. When the coast was clear we crawled across on our stomachs and reached the other side without incident – feeling rather foolish to have taken unnecessary trouble, but relieved that we were getting nearer 'home'.

It was always a puzzle to me that the occupying forces never seemed to use dogs when they were hunting for Partisans or agents like ourselves. I felt sure they could have improved their success rate with a good pack of hounds.

Nor did the Germans ever seem to hide themselves in one area for any length of time to wait for Partisan activity to show itself. They were always so predictable in their searches, arriving in large numbers and combing areas systematically. To be fair to the Germans, clandestine warfare was not as sophisticated as it is today, and methodical searches on a grid system were the approved technique. Nevertheless Keany and I discussed as we headed back how we would have scattered observers under cover for 48 hours at a time if we had been the occupying army trying to mop up resistance groups. What the Germans lacked in flair, they gained in organization, but I always felt our individuality had the edge in situations like this one.

As we tramped back that night, we saw fresh evidence that the search for Partisans and sympathizers had taken its toll. Two of the farmhouses we passed on our return had been reduced to smouldering ruins. This meant that Fascist patrols suspected the occupants of helping our cause. If they ever found positive evidence that a farmer's family had assisted the resistance groups, they would be taken back to German headquarters, tortured and shot. Where no proof existed but suspicion lingered, farms would be put to the torch. The already poor occupiers would be forced to move in with equally poor, overcrowded relatives or friends. Where none existed we would sometimes see families continuing to live in the burnt-out shells of their former homes at the mercy of the elements. They were a pitiful sight.

Such scenes always hardened my attitude towards the enemy and stiffened my resolve not to feel sorry for them again when they were caught in ambushes. At least, I told myself, they were soldiers fighting a war. But these poor Italian peasants were just trying to get on with life as best they could. It was a hard enough struggle for existence at the best of times. To have their homes arbitrarily destroyed on the whim of an invading army was pitiless cruelty.

The Germans and Italian Fascists must have known that, even if they had helped the Partisans, these simple farmers had probably had little choice in the matter. Faced with desperate armed men from either side, the local inhabitants were helpless. Most of them probably did not care who won the war as long as it stopped and these unwelcome strangers went away. Then they could go back to scratching a meagre living and raising their families with only crop failures and animal disease to worry about in future.

Keany and I were convinced that we represented their best hopes of a speedy end to the hostilities.

'It's nearly over now,' said Keany. 'Jerry just wants one last kick up the backside and he'll be out of Italy. I reckon we're the ones to give that boot, Bill.'

We reached the safety of our leaf-lined hut just before dawn, half buried ourselves in the soft foliage, and immediately fell asleep again. Four hours later we awoke, refreshed and ready for another day.

By now the Fascist *rastrellamenti* were at their height. The activity of the patrols leaving Monesiglio had hit a new level of intensity. Keany and I were feeling distinctly uncomfortable. We had heard from our Partisan friends that the Germans knew a British agent was sending radio messages from the area.

We were running out of new places from which to transmit and receive. The Germans had several direction-finding vehicles now and we felt our luck could not last forever. But it was vital we send a message as soon as possible to let our Bari base know we were still in business and to tell them in no uncertain manner that the situation was getting rather hot for us. So, with more caution than usual, we crept out of our hut and headed for the hills once more. Two Partisan scouts had been provided to keep lookout for us as we made our way to a friendly farmhouse. Time and again our leading comrade would wave his hand and we would dart for cover.

Sometimes it was a false alarm, and our guide would emerge sheepishly to carry on the journey, but on one occasion we leapt into a ditch seconds before a patrol of twenty men from the Brigata Nera marched down the track past us. My face was only inches from the muddy boots of these Mussolini supporters as I held my breath and prayed I had not left an untidy limb on view. Fortunately they were soon gone and our S.O.E. training — that keeping absolutely still is the best camouflage — paid off again.

But our close call reminded us that in our situation there was no possibility to chat as we continued on our way. Eventually, after a two-hour journey, we arrived at a small farm building which was to be our transmission site.

One of our guides went 400 yards along the dirt track beyond the farmhouse. The other waited 400 yards short of our destination. There was no sign of the farmer, who had vacated the premises after the leading Partisan had a word in his ear.

As usual I jammed a stone into a loop at the end of 50 feet of copper wire. This was my radio aerial. Then I threw it as high as I could up a tree to maximise the signal strength. The wire was connected to my radio inside the farmhouse and I was in business.

I told Bari I was safe and well with Keany and we were ready for any messages. After I had taken down coded gobbledegook for 15 minutes, I handed the pad for Keany to translate into sense. Meanwhile I sent his coded messages back to Bari.

We had been transmitting for another 15 minutes when the balloon went up. Our excitable Partisan friend came running up the road like an Olympic sprinter with his backside on fire. I did not need to be a keen student of the Italian language and its colourful dialects to get the drift of what he was gabbling at 300 words a minute. He had spotted a German direction-finding vehicle and it was heading straight for us. It would be arriving any minute.

Keany grabbed the batteries. I sent another QUG signal, disconnected the aerial and put the set in my back-pack. We dashed outside, but when I tried to pull the aerial out of the tree, it snagged on one of the branches. The harder I pulled, the firmer it became stuck. By now I was sweating, and it had nothing to do with the temperature. Our guide had gone ahead to tell his comrade to run for it. The courageous Keany stayed to cover me. Every second seemed like an eternity and I could feel a wave of mild hysteria starting to grip me. But I managed to pull myself together with the most supreme mental effort. To leave the tell-tale wire behind would spell almost certain death for the farmer and his family. It would also show the Germans they were hot on our heels. So, after regaining my shattered nerves and patching them together, I became cool and detached again for a few vital seconds. I tried to flick the wire upwards away from the branch which

46

was snagging it. At the second attempt, the wire freed itself and fell at my feet. I grabbed it and ran round the side of the farmhouse just as the German lorry's spluttering exhaust came into earshot.

Keany and I darted into an orchard as I continued to stuff the awkward wire into the pocket of my battledress. We just reached the cover of the first trees in time to look back and see an armoured car halt outside the farm building 100 yards away. A swivel machine gun was mounted on top, attended by a soldier who was scouring the area, using the gun like a searchlight to seek out his quarry. A second armoured car arrived along with the radio direction-finding lorry.

We waited until they were occupied with a search of the building before we made our way through the orchard, hopping from tree to tree. One of our Partisan friends found himself sharing our hide and seek ordeal. I neither knew nor cared at this stage of the operation what had become of our other Italian comrade. I simply assumed that he was making his own arrangements to get the hell out of there.

Each time the German machine gunner on the armoured car turned away from us, we set off deeper into the orchard. Little by little we made our way out of sight. Just before we disappeared from view I saw the Germans questioning the farmer, who had returned to the scene to face the music. He was looking suitably perplexed by the Germans' interrogation and I hoped we had not compromised him in any way. I felt sure that as long as he kept his nerve there was nothing to fear. Easier said than done, perhaps.

Independently Keany, the Partisan and I made our way to the far side of the orchard where we were out of sight of the farmhouse. Then, with a wave of his hand, our Italian scout indicated that he would be making his own way back to his version of civilization.

Keany and I would have to set off alone once again for our hut on the outskirts of Monesiglio. But first we found a 'picnic site' where we could eat the rough bread we had snatched from the farmhouse as we beat our hasty retreat.

As we paused for breath and started to unpack our meagre

rations, Keany exclaimed, 'At last. We're getting out of here.'

He had been deciphering the coded notes we had received from Bari as he munched his bread. Suddenly a smile lit up his face as he was struggling to make sense of the message. After his first outburst, he continued in a more serious manner to decode the message.

'What's going on?' I asked eagerly. 'Where are they sending us?'

'Can you keep a secret?' he asked, grinning. 'We're going to Milan. And we start tomorrow.'

IV

CROSSING THE TORRENT

As darkness fell the following evening, a Partisan courier came by prior arrangement to the Biestros' farmhouse kitchen in Monesiglio. Keany and I had made our way down from our hut on the hillside and we arrived there simultaneously. Then, while Luisa made us a farewell dinner, Keany outlined the plan.

Our guide had been sent by Captain Ballard. He was an ex-Alpini Regiment soldier named Settimo Maggiorino − a man in his late twenties from Mondovi and an accomplished mountaineer who seemed to know every blade of grass in his native Piedmont.

Settimo Maggiorino was dark-haired and of medium build, ever cheerful but passionately conscientious and fervently anti-Fascist. Like many of his comrades in that well-trained regiment, Maggiorino took exception to being ordered around by the Germans. He had never been a fan of Mussolini and took the first opportunity to join the Autonomous Partisans who opposed him.

It was he who was to guide us to an isolated farm where we would link up with Hope, Roccia and Millard. I had already made my broadcast that day, informing Monopoli base that we were alive and well and ready to be on our way. So after warm handshakes and kisses from the Biestros (the kisses were received abundantly from both Tal and Luisa!), Maggiorino led us away into the night. He was casually dressed in blue-grey trousers, sports jacket and open-necked shirt. Like Captain Ballard, his S.O.E. coordinator, Maggiorino looked as if he was on his way to a grouse shoot. But the sub-machine gun swinging at a jaunty angle from his shoulder gave the lie to any such impression.

He took us north of Monesiglio for some five kilometres. We stopped talking whenever we neared farmhouses en route, but still the ubiquitous dogs sensed our presence and howled their displeasure. This made me feel distinctly uneasy, but it failed to rouse the farmers, for I never saw any lights go on as a result of the dogs' noisy protests. I suspect many of those farmers did not want to know what was happening. To them ignorance was bliss. After an hour we reached our destination − another farmhouse where we were reunited with our comrades Hope, Roccia and Millard. There was barely time to exchange greetings before we set off once again for Cisterna.

We were later to swap stories about our respective adventures, but our first priority was to head for the city of Alba, where we were to make a hazardous crossing of the fast-flowing River Tanaro. Maggiorino left behind the other Italian guide who had brought the band of Hope to meet us and we stepped out into the moonless night.

Our first destination was the village of Barbaresco, where we were to meet Pietro Berutti, the 20-year-old son of a local vineyard owner. Pietro was not one of those Partisans who had taken up arms and headed for the hills to fight a guerrilla war against the occupying armies of Fascism. He had taken up a potentially more dangerous role by staying at home and giving all outward appearances of leading the life of a farmer interested only in his grape harvest. Unknown to the German garrison in the nearby city of Alba, Pietro was a staunch supporter of the Partisans and had risked his life countless times by providing food, shelter, directions and, most importantly, a secret crossing of the river.

The Tanaro may be little more than a trickle in the summer for all I know, but during the thaw at the end of winter it was a swollen torrent containing treacherous currents which would swallow the unwary swimmer. Pietro had constructed an ingenious means of crossing the river at a point

5 The author revisits the "hut which was to be our home from home for the next three weeks". (p.28)

6 Pietro and Romana Berutti at their vineyard in 1990: "Pietro was not one of those Partisans who had taken up arms to fight a guerrilla war . . . He had taken up a more dangerous role . . ." (p.50)

less than 100 yards from a bridge. When we arrived after walking for another three hours across rugged country, he was waiting by appointment to lead us to the spot. He pointed out the silhouettes of the Italian Fascist soldiers patrolling the bridge and showed us by example how to cover our white faces with mud. Then he led Hope, Roccia and Millard to a boat which had been cleverly camouflaged by dead branches and leaves. The boat was sheltered from the bridge by a small copse and we saw that a similar cluster of trees awaited us 50 yards away on the distant bank.

I looked at the modest boat and the surging river. I did not fancy its chances one bit. But Pietro had a trick up his sleeve. The boat was linked to a rope which was tied round trees on each bank. Using both hands on the left hand side of the craft, Hope, Roccia and Millard were shown how to haul themselves across to the other side, silently, without oars and in no great danger of being swept away by the current.

The process took some 20 minutes; as they set off, Keany, Maggiorino and myself walked down to the river bank to get into position. As I followed the Captain, every step he took produced a loud fart which seemed to shatter the silence. Perhaps Keany was suffering from nerves and his way of releasing tension set me off giggling like a schoolgirl. For some inexplicable reason the idea of being caught, tortured and shot after all those weeks of planning and all those months of training just because somebody had farted seemed hilariously funny. I told Keany his was an ill wind which was going to get us blown to pieces. Then we both started giggling hysterically.

My comrades were not amused. They urged Keany and I to be quiet and eventually we composed ourselves. When the first group had reached the other side, we helped Pietro to pull himself back for a second journey with us. As we hauled ourselves across, I was afraid to breathe as I saw the enemy soldiers strolling along the bridge nearby. It seemed impossible for them not to see us. Pietro has since explained that he chose the spot deliberately because on moonless nights the crossing point is blanketed by the trees. Although boat passengers could make out the shadowy figures of the guards from the background lights of the town, they could not have seen us even if they had been staring in our direction. I would have appreciated the comfort of that information at the time because I was convinced we would be spotted. My relief when we reached the shelter of the trees on the far bank was tremendous. Pietro wished us a fond farewell and we helped to pull him back to his home shore.

It was 12.30 am as we waved across the bank to him and set off to continue our journey to Cisterna.

By now I was feeling weary. I had been humping my radio set and sub-machine gun for the best part of five hours without a break. But the real stamina-sapper was the nervous tension caused by the danger of crossing the Tanaro. After the initial flood of relief at safely negotiating this hazard, I was now in a state of anti-climax which led to a psychological form of exhaustion.

This sense of torpor was not made any easier by the thought that we now had to tramp for another six hours to reach the castle of Cisterna, which sat atop a 2,000-foot-high hill. The others looked equally grim-faced but determined as the sprightly, disgustingly-fit Maggiorino led the way. His cheerful chatter helped to raise our spirits, although I could not help thinking I would rather be back in the Old Bell at Henley. Being a brave hero was all right in theory, but I had never realized it involved such physical hard work.

We skirted the small town of San Damiano as it lay in darkness and then took the direct route to Cisterna. We were about a mile from the castle when dawn began to break spectacularly over the hillside. Although the mediaeval stone castle was hidden from view, we started to see armed Partisan sentries guarding the passes on the zig-zagging path which wound its way to the castle gates.

Maggiorino had taken a 200-yard lead on the last lap of our journey to warn the guards that we were allies. These brigand-like figures held their rifles aloft to salute us as we passed them.

We rounded the last bend and a straight path led to the castle door. It lacked only a moat and a drawbridge to complete the picture of the sort of fortress from which St George would have emerged to slay dragons. It had a commanding view of the countryside on every compass point for miles around and was regarded as impregnable. The Germans and the Italian Fascists had tried on numerous occasions to take the castle and flush out the Partisans, but every effort had failed. The stronghold was accepted as a fact of life and the occupying forces lived in fear of 'The Bandits of Cisterna', as they called them.

Hundreds of ex-Alpini Regiment troops had flocked to their charismatic leader, Major Enrico Mauri, who led the region's Autonomous Partisans. The 1943 Partisan uprising had occurred like spontaneous combustion as patriotic Italian troops rebelled against the continued German occupation.

I have no doubt the London-based S.O.E. was happy to fan the flames of resistance and supply arms to their former enemy, but it was Major Mauri who moulded them into a formidable fighting force who grew in strength and esteem.

By the time Hope, Millard, Roccia, Keany, Maggiorino and I arrived at the beginning of March, 1945, the bandits of Cisterna were so confident they took it in turns to have Sundays off from the war! The men would wash, shave, get spruced up, go to church and play bowls in the town squares nearby, sometimes under the noses of the unsuspecting Germans. Little did they know that these peaceful bowlers were the fearsome bandits who carried out ambushes on convoys at night and who undermined the Axis war effort with their sabotage of trains, bridges and factories.

Major Mauri's men also held prisoners in their castle who would eventually be exchanged for Partisans who had fallen into German hands. Ironically, many of these German prisoners were reluctant to take part in the swaps because they felt safer in the hands of the Italian resistance movement than they did near the front line of a retreating army. From what I learned, such prisoners were initially subjected to rough treatment and humiliation by the Partisans. But within a few days they were among the happiest soldiers in the Third Reich.

Keany and I spent a couple of days in Cisterna regaining

our strength after our exertions and planning the next stage of our journey to Milan. It was decided we would disguise ourselves as peasants and take a donkey and cart to the far side of the occupied town of Villanova. There we would be met by Partisans on the north of Villanova and taken to meet Gino, a leader with the Justice and Liberty Party. He, in turn, would lead us to his boss Renato, who would guide us to the town of Brusasco. At this stage I was given no more details of the plan. It only remained for us to don our disguises and wait for nightfall.

We must have looked the two most unconvincing peasants ever seen in northern Italy. Keeping on our battledress for warmth and future use, we pulled on pairs of baggy old trousers over the top, fastened with broad belts. Then we added a couple of threadbare jackets with patched elbows from the castle 'wardrobe department'. Our dazzling outfits were completed by the addition of a pair of floppy hats that may have been trilbys in their youth but which had parted company with their headbands much earlier in the century. I felt more like a partygoer at the tramps' ball than a fighting soldier. It was just possible that a blind man on a galloping racehorse might have failed to spot something odd about this strange duo in British army boots masquerading as peasants. But I put all my faith in not meeting anyone at that time of night.

The Partisans loaded our cart with root vegetables resembling turnips. These covered my radio transmitter. We placed our sub-machine guns out of sight at the front of the cart where they were within speedy reach in the event of trouble.

Because of the steepness of the path heading down from the castle we were obliged to lead the donkey and his load away while walking alongside the obliging creature. Hope, Roccia and Millard joined Major Mauri in wishing us 'Bon Voyage'.

Keany was laughing as usual as we set off at dusk.

'To be sure and aren't I feeling at home now,' he said with an exaggerated bog Irish accent. 'These vehicles are all the rage in County Cork.'

After a mile the road to Villanova flattened out gradually. Keany and I then took turns to ride the cart while the other walked. We never saw the sentries who guarded the route to the castle, but we never doubted they were there.

It was about midnight as we approached the tiny town. In the distance I heard a train coming from our right as we headed for the bridge which would carry us over the line to the main street.

'Perfect spot for a bit of sabotage,' I observed to Keany.

'No time for distraction,' he replied. 'We can't afford to draw attention to ourselves.'

It was too late for us to do anything anyway. The train passed through the town as we passed over the railway bridge. But 200 yards along the track we heard a huge explosion and a blinding flash illuminated the sky.

'Sweet Jaysus,' said Keany, this time in a genuine Irish accent. 'Let's get the hell out of here.'

We spurred the donkey into top gear and raced through the town as fast as we could, shedding turnips as we made haste along the bumpy roads. It seemed a group of Partisans had also decided this was a nice spot for a derailment and had blown up the train.

Not knowing whether it was carrying troops or whether the explosion would bring reinforcements to the area, we decided to spend no time sightseeing in Villanova. We were clear of the main street by the time its lights started to flicker on as the townsfolk peered out to see what had happened.

Our donkey was as startled as we were by the explosion, and happy to heed our promptings as we put as much distance as possible between ourselves and its source. We had left the town behind us and were just beginning to feel secure again as we continued north.

Then, from a few yards away in the darkness, a voice shouted in authoritative Italian: 'Stop. Put your hands in the air and do not move.'

Instinctively I pulled on the reins to stop my fiery steed. Keany, who had been trotting alongside the cart, stopped and put his hands casually into the air. I took my cue from him and followed suit.

'Leave this to me,' he whispered out of the corner of his mouth.

For what seemed like an eternity, and what was actually only a few seconds, we waited like a frozen tableau. Even our donkey seemed rooted to the spot. All sorts of pessimistic possibilities flashed through my mind as I peered out into the darkness to distinguish our captors.

My great fear was that they would prove to be Italian Fascists and that we would be suspected of blowing up the troop train at Villanova. If this was the case, it would take only the flimsiest of searches to discover that we were wearing British battledress under our peasants' garb. A further search would then reveal the radio and the two sub-machine guns. Could we feign astonishment at their discovery? Pretend to wonder who on earth put them there? Cast suspicion on the donkey? I thought not.

As my mind raced it became clear we had two choices: make a grab for our weapons and risk almost certain and instant death; or wait and hope for the best. Happily, Keany, with the luck of the Irish, made the right decision and our prayers were answered. From the hedgerows at the side of the road six men emerged simultaneously with an assorted collection of pistols, rifles and sub-machine guns trained on us. When they drew nearer I could see the now familiar brigands' costumes and the distinctive red neckerchiefs.

We had been captured by the Garibaldini. The gravest danger — that they might have been a Fascist patrol — had passed. But we were by no means home and dry. The same voice which had ordered us to halt now addressed us again in Italian as its user approached us. He was obviously their leader and he aimed his first question at me.

'Who are you and where are you going?' he demanded in Italian.

Keany answered for me. 'We are British soldiers,' he said, first in English, then in Italian.

The leader of the Communist Partisans grinned, revealing a set of gleaming white teeth from which the main group of four were missing. He prodded Keany in the chest with his gun and said sarcastically: 'I don't think much of your new uniforms.'

With this, the other men laughed and I was given an unfriendly prod by a man with a pistol. Keany kept his nerve and for an Irishman showed all the characteristics of a British officer maintaining a stiff upper lip in the face of adversity. He spoke excellent Italian because of his war efforts against them in Abyssinia.

'Don't prod me, my friend, or you may lose some more teeth,' he said. The gap-toothed grin vanished from the face of the Garibaldini leader and my heart sank. To think that prior to the war Keany had been embarking on a career in the diplomatic service. But before our captors could react to his comment, Keany gave his warmest smile.

'My comrade and I are on a secret mission which will help kick Adolf and his Fascist pigs out of Italy and all the way back to Berlin,' he announced.

This remark seemed to relax the Communist leader, whose men followed his example in everything. He opened Keany's shirt, studied his battledress and examined his boots.

'You have cigarettes?' he demanded.

'We certainly do,' said Keany, still smiling and extending his right hand to shake that of the Partisan boss, while respectfully keeping the other aloft.

The Garibaldini chief took his hand, smiled, shook it and a wave of relief swept over me.

'Give them a packet each, Billy boy,' said Keany in English. At pistol point I was allowed to fumble through my peasant shirt into the pockets of my battledress. Like a third rate magician, I kept producing packets of Gold Flake from different compartments.

'Here you are, comrade,' I said in my best Italian as I handed the booty around. The sight of the English cigarettes helped to back up our story and each of the Italians lowered his weapon while he enjoyed a smoke. Keany and I lit up as well to consolidate the feeling of togetherness and comradeship.

'Where are you going?' another of the Garibaldini asked.

'It's best you don't know,' said Keany. 'We're meeting

some of your country cousins from the Justice and Liberty group eventually. But our mission is top secret.'

Then he explained how a troop train had been blown up at Villanova and how angry Fascists could soon be heading in our direction. The Garibaldini gave me a drink from their wine flasks as Keany talked to their leader.

Our friendly chat took an unpleasant turn, however, when one of the Partisans discovered my Marlin lying under the turnips. He wanted to keep it and offered me his World War One pistol in exchange. One of his comrades then uncovered Keany's sub-machine gun and my radio.

This seemed to remind their leader that the Allies had let them down with the supply of weapons. The sight of two modern sub-machine guns and a radio transmitter must have been the equivalent of strawberries to our donkey.

Keany sensed the danger and asked him in great detail what arms they needed and how they could be contacted to get ready for the drop. The boss of the Garibaldini group made an outrageous request for enough weapons to equip a dozen divisions.

Without a flicker of emotion, Keany dutifully noted the precise requirements. Then he asked the Italian what would help in the way of food, clothes, blankets and ammunition. The eager Communist made similar extravagant claims for supplies which the captain scribbled down gravely in his pocket book.

Then Keany took elaborate details of how a plane could signal as it went over a dropping point on one night, and the Garibaldini would light special flares to show the supplies target for the next night. My Irish comrade took scrupulous notes, occasionally suggesting improvements to the plan.

Keany supervised the reloading of our weapons and radio on to the cart, gave handshakes all round and a final warning about the possibility of enemy troops approaching from Villanova. There were further promises of 'See you in Milan on Liberation Day' and words to that effect before we set off once more going north away from Villanova.

The Garibaldini headed south-eastwards down a farm

track as we clattered away with Keany holding the reins while I quick-marched alongside him.

After 200 yards or so I remarked, 'How on earth are you going to persuade HQ to send all those weapons and supplies to the Reds?'

Keany laughed and took out his pocket book. He ripped out the three pages of notes he had just made, rolled them into a small ball and tossed it over the hedge.

'I don't know what you're talking about,' he said with his most disarming smile.

An hour later we parked our donkey and cart near another of the isolated farmhouses which provided food and accommodation for the Partisans and their allies. Keany had used a prearranged series of flashlight signals to announce our arrival and had received the appropriate response in return.

So we joined two new Partisan comrades and tucked into plates of polenta provided by the farmer's wife. Then we four retired for the night to a farm outbuilding with our weapons and radio.

Although the farmer and his wife could have allowed us to stay inside, they explained cheerfully that if we were caught while we slept that night they could deny all knowledge of our existence. We were told there were intensive *rastrellamenti* in the Montafia area where we were staying, as more and more Italians were deserting the Republican Army and joining the Partisans. It was like trying to turn back the tide for the German occupiers. The more Italian soldiers who joined the Partisans, the stronger they became and the more prisoners they captured. These prisoners would often be happy to change sides without too much persuasion.

Despite the propaganda war, it was becoming increasingly obvious that ordinary Italians wanted the occupying German forces to leave. The Partisans and their British and American allies provided the best means to achieve this. But the Germans and the dwindling numbers of Italian Republicans were determined and well-trained troops.

They were now making one last-ditch effort to assert themselves with detailed searches which would mop up

Partisan resistance before the formidable forces of the main allied army poured remorselessly northwards through Italy.

So as we grabbed three hours sleep before dawn, Keany and I were left in little doubt that although the war was drawing towards its inevitable conclusion, the danger to us was increasing. This sobering thought was still with us at daybreak as we set off to join a division of the Justice and Liberty faction of the resistance forces. Still dressed as peasants, we were led to a hillside and introduced to Gino, the right-hand man of Renato, their divisional commander. Gino was with a group of some 120 mountain men. They looked like gipsies with bandoliers over their shoulders, but they proved to be a highly disciplined and dedicated band of soldiers.

Among them was a prisoner they had recently taken at pistol-point from one of the nearby occupied villages. He was a sergeant in the S.S. Keany knew a few phrases of German so he questioned him about troop movements and plans. The German sergeant was not bound or gagged. He was free to roam around within the group of Partisans during the daytime, sharing their standard meals of bread, raw eggs and red wine, but he was under no illusions as to what would happen to him should he try to escape. He knew there would be no second chances and his best hope for survival was a speedy end to the war or an exchange for Partisan prisoners.

The German was a good soldier and he refused to betray any secrets to Keany beyond his name, rank and number. He received better treatment than Italian prisoners captured by the Partisans, who tended to be beaten and abused for helping the Fascist dictators to rule their country. I suspect he was a more valuable commodity when exchanges were made, so perhaps they were keeping him in mint condition.

After our early lunch with Gino and his merry men, we all set off across the hillside to link up with Renato, who had the plans for the next stage of our journey. Scouts were sent on ahead as we tramped through the rough terrain towards our invisible goal.

Gino explained that we might reach Renato before nightfall providing we managed to avoid any enemy patrols. The words were hardly out of his mouth when two scouts came running towards us at breakneck speed waving us back towards a row of handily placed bushes. Obeying the scouts' signals without question, we did not have to wait long to find the reason for their panic. As we lay behind the bushes we had a clear view of a ridge 100 yards away, slightly below our line of vision. We had only just settled ourselves when a patrol of thirty blue-uniformed Republicans marched into sight along the ridge. It was a tempting target. But as the first platoon passed under the barrels of our loaded guns, a second platoon hove into view. The first group of soldiers headed for a small collection of houses, cottages and sprawling farms which formed a hamlet a few hundred yards from our position. As the second platoon set off to follow them, a third group appeared. They were followed by platoons four, five and six, making a total of 180 men, who made a thorough search of the tiny village. Little did they know that the objects of their search had them covered every inch of the way.

There was much wringing of hands by the villagers as the Fascist patrol turned their search into a provocative piece of intimidation. We could hear the sound of glass and crockery being smashed by the clumsy soldiers and the muted protests of the glowering peasants. Eventually the platoons marched away northwards in the direction which we would eventually be taking.

As soon as they were out of sight and earshot, Keany launched into a furious tirade against our comrades. As they got up from behind the screen of bushes, Keany was marching up and down in front of them, screaming in Italian:

'You call yourselves men. Why did you let such an opportunity pass? We could have ambushed those Fascists. You are here to fight the enemy, not hide behind bushes like frightened women.'

On and on he ranted as the expression on the Partisans' faces changed from bewilderment to anger. I could not begin to understand Keany's logic. It was true we had the drop on the Republicans and we could have taken them by surprise, but they were all well armed and most of them would have survived our initial burst. Then what were we going to do?

They could have called up reinforcements from throughout the region. Bushes were no protection against bullets and we would have been forced to retreat in the opposite direction from where we were heading.

Gino was most indignant. He explained that the philosophy of guerrilla warfare was to hit and run, not to stand and fight. In normal circumstances, said Gino, they might have opened fire and then made a quick tactical withdrawal.

'But we are under orders to evade the enemy,' said Gino with a hurt expression. 'We have been told that we must accompany you to Renato and that nothing must detract us from our main purpose.'

Keany was unrepentant. He refused to accept the sensible attitude of the Partisans in staying clear of danger for our sakes. I could understand his frustration because he was a man of action and we seemed to have spent the entire mission so far in avoiding it. Nevertheless there was no excuse for his rudeness and his implications of cowardice to men who were risking their lives every moment of every day for their cause.

Gino and his men sulked for a while after Keany's outburst, but they were professional enough not to let it interfere with the job in hand. We waited an hour and then followed the same path which the Fascists had taken, with scouts going on ahead to make sure we did not catch up with them.

At 5 pm I made our radio broadcast to tell HQ we had safely negotiated Villanova and that we were on our way with Gino to meet Renato. We also described our close encounter with the Fascists and the subsequent delay to our meeting with Renato, which would now take place tomorrow.

As darkness fell we gave away our peasant clothes and floppy hats to the Partisans for their 'wardrobe department'. There was nothing to eat that night, which we spent on the open hillside.

V

AMBUSHED

On the morning of 8 March, 1945, there was no sign of imminent doom or disaster. There were no dark, brooding storm clouds in the sky or any of the other legendary portents to warn us. In fact it was a cool, crisp day of clear blue skies when we awoke around 6 am.

Keany and I had slept huddled together for warmth beneath a bush. We each had blankets to keep the dew off our battledress. All around us pairs of swarthy Partisans were emerging from similar bushes where they had spent the night like young lovers, snuggling up to retain their body heat.

By now we were ravenously hungry, having had nothing since our raw eggs and bread the previous afternoon. But we knew there was no immediate respite for our complaining stomachs. We were in rough open country and there was no hope of food until we found a friendly farmhouse. Even then we were likely to be on short rations. The prospect of a poor farmer having enough provisions put by to feed 120 hungry mouths was worse than remote. So we all had a swig of red wine from our flasks and tried to ignore our grumbling stomachs.

We carried out our ritual ablutions and surveyed the scene as dawn crept over the hillsides. It was clear from scores of messengers and from the evidence of our own eyes that the enemy was all around us.

The Germans and Italian Fascists were carrying out a series of thorough *rastrellamenti* in our area north of Villanova d'Asti. Thousands of them were combing the district by foot, cycle, motor-bike, jeep and truck looking for Partisans in general and the Englishman with the radio transmitter in particular.

I had visions of seeing my face on some Western-style poster above the words: 'Wanted: Dead or Alive – Billy the Kid.'

We were reasonably safe at night, but by day our lives were in constant danger. It is a natural human feeling to find safety in numbers. Keany and I were delighted after spending so long in isolation to be with such a large band of allies. On the other side of the coin, groups of 120 armed men tend to attract more attention than two. Consequently our joy at being with Gino and his men from the Partisans' Justice and Liberty Party was diluted by our knowledge that we could not move in the daytime without being noticed.

The hated German S.S., many of whom were Mongols from Russia, and the dreaded Italian Brigata Nera (Black Brigade) were ruthless in their dealings with the villagers, farmers and peasants. They treated any surliness with brutality. If there was the slightest evidence that a farmhouse or home had been used to harbour Partisans, it was burnt to the ground.

Despite our popular support, we were therefore under no illusions that a frightened farmer might betray us just as well as a Fascist supporter. Moving by daylight was a hazardous business which was best kept to a minimum. Nevertheless Keany and I were needed in Milan as soon as possible to help with its liberation. Our first stop was to be Brusasco, one third of the way between Cisterna and Milan. The overall plan was to go to the house of Dr Ferrero Burrino, an active Partisan supporter, who would hide us in his house and then drive us in his car to sympathizers in Milan. The drive from Brusasco to Milan would be a deadly gamble – a calculated risk which would result in complete success or total failure. But the most difficult part of the journey was the route to Brusasco from our present position just north of Villanova. We knew from yesterday's close encounter with the Italian Fascist patrol that the enemy could be hiding behind every tree, bush or hedgerow between here and our destination.

Gino sent scouts ahead and led us to his commander, Renato, to decide the best method of reaching Brusasco some 15 miles away. We walked for the best part of a mile with Gino's 120-strong group before we spotted the young leader of the region's Justice and Liberty Party.

Renato was a tall university-educated Italian from the Piedmont Province. He exuded a quiet authority and had a calming influence over some of his more excitable, arm-waving junior officers. He awaited our arrival by arrangement on the northern end of a long hill with 20 of his own men. Introductions were made and I was left to chat as best I could with the lower ranks while Keany and Renato took part in an animated conversation with the other leaders.

Renato, wearing a British battledress jacket, was obviously at odds with Keany over what we should do. He had promised to send a guide with us to Brusasco, but wanted to wait for the cover of darkness before we set off in that direction. He was also keen to move back from the hill where our presence in such large numbers might be spotted by our invisible enemy using field glasses. Keany's argument was on the lines that, as we were in constant danger anyway, we might as well keep moving towards the comparative safety of Dr Burrino in Brusasco.

'You're showing too much respect for the enemy,' Keany told Renato. 'I'd sooner be shot at going forward rather than standing still or retreating. Let's push on.'

With dignified coolness, Renato replied, 'Be sensible and trust me. I haven't survived this long in these hills by just running away from danger. There's a time to go forward and a time to go back. Right now it's time to go back off this hill.'

Keany would not listen to this negative train of thought. 'How do we know we won't walk back into an enemy patrol,' he argued. 'There's just as much chance of that happening if we go back as if we go forward.'

Renato, Gino and his senior officers conferred once more. At last a compromise was reached. Gino and some 120 men would go back off the hill. Keany, Renato and I would remain with about twenty Partisans and keep low until we thought the coast was clear.

As Gino and his men pulled out at 9 a.m., I noticed a couple of German soldiers entering a farm building a mile below us. There was no great significance in this, because the Germans and the Italian Fascists were searching the entire area. We were reasonably confident that, from our vantage point on the hill, we could observe the enemy without their seeing us. But when I saw another small group of Germans enter the same building, I became uneasy. I knew that if they had seen us through binoculars, they were not likely to mistake us for a shepherds' convention.

'What's going on?' I asked Keany as we observed the activity at the farmyard.

'They're probably having some breakfast, the lucky sods,' said Keany, massaging his rumbling tummy and licking his lips.

Keany carried on chatting to Renato about our route to Brusasco and the prospects of food on the way. My remark had only served to remind us all of our hunger. I chatted meanwhile with a Partisan from Calabria who joined me in a smoke. He was sporting a German Luger pistol which he had captured during an ambush. He tried to sound matter-of-fact about his acquisition of the weapon, but it was obviously a treasured possession and a badge of honour to him.

As we chatted I noticed more knots of Germans entering the farm building. I was becoming increasingly uneasy. Something from my days of playing Cowboys and Indians round Oldham and Manchester warned me that all was not well.

Renato left Keany to tell his men what had been decided and I walked over to my comrade to express my fears.

'I don't like this one little bit,' I said with as much urgency as I could muster. 'It's those Germans down there. I haven't seen sight or sound of them since they went into that building.'

'You worry too much,' said the ever-confident Keany. 'They don't enjoy scouring the countryside looking for Partisans and wondering when they might get ambushed. They're probably just skiving off and keeping out of harm's way for a while.'

I remained unconvinced. 'But it doesn't make sense,' I insisted. 'During the past two hours I've seen about sixty Germans go in that building in threes and fours. I haven't seen one come out. If you ask me, they've spotted us and they're creeping up to attack us.'

There was not a sound or a sight to back up my claim, just a sixth sense which told me we were in mortal danger. I was naturally more pessimistic than the courageous Keany, but on this occasion there was an extra intangible ingredient to my wariness.

Keany said, 'Don't be silly Bill. They couldn't creep up a hill like this without us seeing or hearing them.'

To the best of my recollection, those were Keany's last words. I had been standing by his side as we spoke, with my radio transmitter in a pack on my back and my Marlin slung over my shoulder. For no reason I could ever explain I suddenly felt frightened, vulnerable and exposed. I moved two or three paces away from Keany's left side back towards the Calabrian and another Partisan called Tony. As I did so the German sub-machine guns opened up. I flung myself to the ground and saw Keany's chest neatly stitched with a row of bullets. He was flung backwards without making a sound, at least no sound which could be heard above the noise of gunfire.

Four other Partisans had been cut down by the initial burst from another sub-machine gun to our right. The rest of us hurled ourselves full length on to our stomachs as the bullets whistled inches overhead.

When Keany was hit I felt the draught from at least three rounds as they zipped past my right ear. At this point all that tedious discipline came into action as army training took over from sheer blind terror and panic. Everything that happened next did so without any conscious pause for thought or consideration. First I loosed off several rounds from my Marlin in the general direction of the enemy guns. I did not expect to hit anybody, but I knew instinctively that a soldier

67

under fire does not aim as accurately as a man whose life is in no danger.

The Calabrian, Tony, and another Partisan named Gino on my left, followed my example and we sent a hail of bullets into the hillside below us. Then I motioned for the Calabrian to fire a burst while I scampered round on my hands and knees to get behind him. I fired a burst and he crawled at top speed to the other side of Tony. Then the Calabrian gave covering fire while Tony dashed to the far side of Gino.

In this way, by keeping the Germans' heads down and running like hell, we retreated off the hill. We were reminded to watch our right flank by the sight of the bodies of our lifeless comrades who had been taken in the first burst of fire.

As we fell back, the German bullets were getting higher over our heads, so we judged that they were taking more time to move up to the crest of the hill than we were taking to scamper away from it. Whether it was our fear or our geographical advantage which benefited us most was hard to tell, but as we escaped from the immediate danger, we ran into more trouble from an attack on our left flank. Germans with sub-machine guns were hiding behind trees as we ran down the slope. They were 200 yards away but well within firing range.

Tony was the first to draw their fire as he ran around Gino. The earth at his feet seemed to leap into life as bullets ripped into it. Immediately, our attention turned from the threat ahead of us and to our right flank to the left side as we pulled back. For a few agonising moments we were pinned down. We knew it was impossible to stay flat on our faces behind what little cover was available. In a few more seconds the Germans ahead of us would have reached the top of the ridge. Then they could pour bullets into us from the other direction.

In the cowboy movies I had watched as a child, this was the time when the 7th Cavalry arrived on the scene with bugles blaring and sabres flashing. On this occasion it was Renato who came to the rescue without any fanfare of trumpets, just his usual calm efficiency.

Although we were pinned down, we could see where our problem lay. A platoon of German soldiers with sub-machine guns and rifles were in a small copse on our left flank 200 yards away. They were firing from behind the cover of the trees.

Renato and his men had got across to the shelter of some trees on our hill a minute or two before us, running at full pelt as soon as the first shots were fired. They had either reached cover before the Germans were in position, or they had run past the danger point with unexpected speed. In either event they were now our saviours as they poured a hail of withering fire into the trees where the Germans were hiding.

Above the infernal din, I heard Renato shout in Italian and then in broken English, 'Over here, Bill.'

He was standing beside a tree stump, looking cool as a cucumber, taking careful aim at the enemy. I saw one of them fall and used that moment to scurry towards a group of trees and stumps which Renato and his men were using as protection.

Just before I started running, I sprayed a burst of sub-machine gun fire at the woods and had time to see another German knocked backwards before I turned and sprinted towards Renato like a demented goat.

In all the excitement I had lost my pistol and my radio battery. But the radio itself was still intact in my back pack. I was later commended for the way I had kept my radio despite coming under heavy fire. It was tempting to shed 12 pounds of excess baggage as we fled, but the truth is that I was terrified of losing that radio. It was my one link with England and I would have felt lost without it. So it was fear, not courage, which caused me to hang on to my precious radio transmitter. Of course in the long term it proved to be a priceless piece of equipment with which we kept head-quarters informed of developments. But I had more selfish reasons for wanting to keep it.

When the Calabrian, Gino, Tony and I joined Renato and a dozen others behind the tree stumps, we provided cover while they climbed a gentle hill behind us. We kept the Germans' heads down while they scrambled to the shoulder of the hill.

Bullets were flying thick and fast now from both sides and we could clearly hear them fizzing through the air. But the shooting was now more general in direction as the opposing forces tried to negate any precision sniping. A couple more Germans fell in the woods and I gained the impression that our shooting was superior.

When Renato reached the shoulder of the hill he got his men behind rocks and boulders. Then he shouted in Italian, 'I'm counting to three. Then we'll cover you. As soon as we start, run like hell.'

I didn't really need telling how fast to run. As soon as Renato's men started their burst, the four of us were haring towards them. By taking it in turns to fire or load, they kept up the covering fire for thirty life-saving seconds.

This gave the four of us time to race below them and round the shoulder of the hill out of the line of fire. After a few seconds to regain our breath, we knew we now had to do the same for Renato's group. We crept back a few feet so we could just aim at the Germans.

Then I shouted in my best Italian, 'On the count of three, we'll start firing. Run for your lives.'

Gino, Tony, the Calabrian and I were now in perfect harmony despite our language difficulties. We knew instinctively what to do as trained soldiers, albeit trained in different armies.

We had led charmed lives during our retreat. After losing five men in the initial ambush, our group had taken no further casualties. The only flaw in our copybook withdrawal came when my Marlin jammed. I had forgotten to clean it for some time because of my preoccupation with the radio, and I paid the penalty when we were in the thick of the action. As I hid behind a tree stump after joining Renato's covering group, my gun refused to fire. It happened as the Germans were advancing towards us from the ridge we had left. I lay down behind the stump and waited for the Germans to advance closer. Renato was standing up fearlessly and picking them off, apparently unimpressed with their return fire.

A blond German was waving on his comrades and I took careful aim at him. I reckoned that if their leader fell, the others would be discouraged. A great idea. What a pity I had not cleaned my gun! As the proud Aryan came into my sights, I squeezed the trigger to fire a burst which would have ended his war instantly. Instead the gun just locked solid. The firing pin would not hit the bullet. Fortunately Renato, by now my hero, took care of him with a well-aimed volley. This gave me time to remove the magazine, get the jammed bullet out and clean the grit from the breech mechanism with a handkerchief to bring the Marlin back into action.

Now we were temporarily out of the line of fire, we could turn our backs on the enemy and run at the double for one third of a mile. Every 50 yards the front man would stop to cover our rear while the others swept past him.

The hill eventually flattened out and we headed for a 50-yard stretch of open land. As we started to cross a heavy machine gun opened up on our left flank. We dived to the ground and scrambled for cover. Our two front runners managed to reach the far side, which was marginally nearer for them. The rest of us, some fourteen strong, crawled back to regroup.

Renato told us we would have to take the risk and cross this treacherous piece of flat ground. 'We have no choice,' he explained. 'If we stay here we die.'

A speedy democratic decision was taken that we should pair up into twos and sprint across. As the first pair raced through the funnel of fire, the next duo set off.

Renato had worked out that the German heavy machine gun was about half a mile away, but within comfortable range to mow us down. As each pair got safely across, I wondered which couple were going to be the unlucky ones. We must have presented an opportunity like flying ducks on a rifle range to the German machine gunners. But on this occasion they failed to win any prizes.

I was the last across with Gino, and, despite putting up

overweight with my radio backpack, I doubt I have ever covered 50 yards in so short a time before or since. When we reached the safety of a head-high ridge on the other side, Gino and I collapsed in an exhausted heap. I sat down and sweat oozed from every pore of my body. This had nothing to do with the heat or the unaccustomed exercise.

It was the first occasion I had had time to stop and think about what had happened in the past three-quarters of an hour, how close I had been to death and how I had lost my closest comrade, Captain John Keany. His belief in his own invincibility had been misplaced and the British Army had lost one of its bravest soldiers.

As this and a thousand other thoughts flashed through my mind, an uncontrollable shaking swept over my whole body. For 45 minutes I had been a man of action, risking life and limb for his country. Now I was a frightened young lad a long way from home.

My plight was made worse because I had lost the only natural English speaker in our group. So I had nobody with whom I could share in detail my private thoughts at that moment. Perhaps it was for the best from a military point of view. This was no time for brooding or reflecting.

We were still in grave danger, with enemy troops only half a mile away and another group presumably closing in on us. It was also fair to assume that reinforcements would be brought into the area as the Germans tried to tighten the net around us.

I had little option but to put all my faith in Renato, with his intimate knowledge of the area. After a brief pause for breath and a swig of red wine, we were on our way again. Renato sent two scouts ahead of us and told us to maintain absolute silence as we continued at first in the same direction. We progressed at walking pace across hills, fields, streams and hedgerows. I had no idea where we were going.

After 20 minutes the two scouts came racing back towards us and motioned for us to take cover. We were lucky enough to be passing a high-banked stream at the time. Our party divided itself between a rocky outcrop and the shallow stream as a German half-track came trundling over the horizon. We watched and waited as it went between us and round a shoulder of hillside out of sight. Renato held a whispered conversation with the scouts and then led us along the precise path which the German half-track had taken. By now I could understand Renato's thinking. It tied in with what the farmer and his wife had told us at Monesiglio about Teutonic efficiency. We were using that systematic approach against them again. The half-track would have radioed its position and reported no sign of us along its route. So we could travel along that route in the opposite direction with some confidence.

For an hour this ploy worked — until our scouts stumbled on a patrol going across our path. One of the scouts had just crept over a stile when a platoon of Republicans from the Decima Mas — ex-Motor Torpedo Boatmen from the defunct Italian Navy — came marching over the brow of a hill along a farm track. He was unable to recross the stile to warn us and we were walking straight into the arms of the enemy. But our Trappist-like vows of silence paid off and saved our skins. We heard the marching Fascists before they heard us and we managed to duck out of sight behind the hedgerow. Through the twigs we could see our scout right in front of us lying face down in a muddy puddle, trying to look invisible. It seemed impossible to me that the Italians could miss him. We all eased off our safety catches and prepared to open fire if necessary. But by keeping his nerve and lying motionless, our scout went unnoticed. His companion, we learned later, was stranded equally helplessly on the far side of the farm track. He had been unable to get back to warn us either, and was ready to attack the platoon from their left flank. This could probably have won the day for us if there had been a fight, but the noise would have brought all the enemy down on us like a ton of bricks. We were happy, therefore, to congratulate our muddy companion for his quick-thinking. Our gratitude stopped short of embraces, however, because the smell from our scout indicated that the track had been much used by farm animals and he was covered in something more than just mud.

We seemed to have been going in no particular direction

up to this point. Our only purpose was to avoid further contact with the enemy. But as the light started to fade Renato decided we should double back towards the hill where we had first come under attack. Again, he never explained his decision at the time. But I could see his logic. The Germans would assume the hill would be the last place on earth we would head for after their ambush. Even if they thought we had spent the last few hours in stationary hiding and we were still in the area, they would be looking inward rather than outward. They would never expect the Partisans they had attacked in overwhelming numbers to be heading in their direction. And the chances were that they would dismiss such a notion as illogical and pull out altogether.

Renato seemed to have guessed right. As darkness fell, we grew more confident and our scouts led us to a friendly farmhouse. Whether the farmer was a genuine sympathizer or whether the sight of sixteen desperate armed men made him so, I was unsure, but he provided a humble fare of scrambled egg and dry bread which was one of the finest meals I have ever eaten. It was our first food in 24 hours. Washed down with the ubiquitous red wine of the region, it was like a feast to us. By now relief had been followed by exhaustion. I assume Renato posted sentries, but I was past caring. After a circuitous hike of some 40 miles, partially under gunfire, with a 12-pound radio on my back, I could not keep my eyes open a moment longer.

The farmer showed us to his stables. With his cows for company, I fell asleep immediately and no Hollywood starlet, Winston Churchill or King George VI himself could have roused me. It was nearly ten hours later when my Partisan comrades finally brought me back to life with a bucket of cold water.

There was no breakfast for us. The farmer apologised and explained we had eaten all his food for supper the night before. So there was only time for our usual swig of red wine from our newly-filled flasks and we were on our way again.

Using two scouts once more, Renato led us cautiously back to the fateful hill where we had been ambushed. Despite our careful approach, it took us only one hour to get there from the shippon where we had enjoyed bed without breakfast.

I found Keany lying as I had last seen him on his back. A neat row of six bullet holes had been stitched diagonally across his chest. We checked for booby traps on Keany and the other Partisans, but they were all clear. However, the Germans had emptied their pockets of any money or valuables, and taken their weapons. I knew Keany had been carrying £2,500 worth of Italian lira − a small fortune in those days − in his back pack. This was to pay for food, ammunition, petrol and information. But the money and the hand generator he had been toting for my radio batteries were missing.

Additionally, the one-time pads containing my code, and the quartz crystals with set wavelengths, had been seen by the enemy, but they had not been removed from his back pack and the chances were that the Germans had failed to appreciate their significance in the search for tangible loot. Nevertheless, I was later told to change both my code and my wavelengths because our situation could have been compromised if the Germans had copied the information.

Seeing Keany and the four Partisans lying there dead on that hillside had an emotionally numbing effect upon me. In the past 24 hours I had become something of a fatalist. Tears do not come easily to me, and I shed none for the courageous Captain, even though I sadly mourned his passing. Whether the British stiff upper lip is a natural inherent phenomenon, or whether we are trained from birth to keep up that image, I do not know. I can only confess that my sorrow at my friend's death was mingled with selfish thanks that I was not lying there in his place. In that situation our cynical thoughts were on the lines: 'Here's to the next man who dies. Let's hope it isn't me.' My Partisan colleagues seemed to feel the same about their fallen comrades. We all knew that death was lurking just around the corner for any of us. When it came, so suddenly, it was a shock to remind us of the peril we were facing constantly. Yet it was no surprise, and to the Partisans it was nothing new. They had learned to bury their dead with quiet dignity and get on with their fight for liberty. So it was on this occasion. Arrangements were made for local villagers to collect the bodies and give them a secret, but decent, Christian burial. The last time I saw Keany's body it was on the back of a donkey cart being led off the hillside by a peasant.

We were told subsequently that the bodies of Keany and the four Partisans had been buried in unmarked graves at Cinaglio and that a sympathetic priest had prayed for their immortal souls.

Keany's lamentable death was now a thing of the past, and our immediate concern was for the future — my own future in particular.

'I can still try to get you to Brusasco,' said Renato. 'One of my men could take you there.'

But I realised there was no point in my pushing on to Brusasco and then making for Milan as originally planned. My whole purpose was to get messages to and from Keany. He alone knew what the overall plan was and he had not confided in me. Working on the 'need-to-know' basis, the good Captain had not burdened me with any secrets in case I had been caught, tortured and forced to tell the enemy our plans. But now, with Keany dead, I was in no position to know what was expected of him.

The million dollar question was whether I should go on to Milan to help Major Max Salvadori. Had Salvadori got separate plans and his own radio operator? If so, would I then be little more than a nuisance — a spare agent whom the Partisans would have to hide? Was it worth the risk to my guide and to Dr Ferrero Burrino in Brusasco to take me to Milan only to find I was not needed?

'It's a long way to go to find I'm surplus to requirements,' I told Renato after much consideration. 'Your guide would be at risk and so would the doctor. Then I might find I'm more trouble than I'm worth to the Partisans in Milan. I reckon that if it was important for me to go to Milan even without Keany, then he would have given me some instructions about what to do if he copped it. The fact that he didn't do so probably means that I was only required there if Keany made it too.'

Renato could see the sense of what I was saying.

'If they need you in Milan,' he said, 'I will risk as many lives as necessary to get you there. But you are quite right. First we must find out whether you are still needed in Milan. And if you are no longer wanted there, you will certainly be useful in Cisterna. They have been having trouble getting radio messages in and out. Let's get you back to Cisterna straight away and find out what your leaders want you to do.'

Renato then had an earnest conversation with one of his men, who left our group on the hillside. An hour later my transport to Cisterna arrived in the shape of a rugged motorbike.

Its rider, Bruno, who spoke not a word of English, was a young peasant. He wore no helmet or hat, but was obviously proud of his enormous leather gauntlets. His rifle was slung over his shoulder, which did little to add to my comfort. Sitting behind him on the pillion seat, I had my 12-pound radio pack and the Marlin weighing me down as I tried to grasp his waist without getting my teeth knocked out by his rifle. We discovered that a passionate embrace keeping the rifle wedged between us was the best way to proceed.

After a short practice circuit I shook hands with Renato and his men, who shouted 'Good luck' in their best English as we set off for Cisterna. We were aware that the area was teeming with enemy troops between Villanova and our destination, but at least we had a chance to get away quickly if we blundered into them.

I clung on tightly as we roared off across the fields. From time to time Bruno would turn and say something in Italian, but I could only nod grimly. Whatever he was telling me was lost in the engine noise or in the translation. Along bumpy farm tracks, down remote lanes and across sloping meadows we travelled. There was no apparent pattern to our journey at first as we twisted first one way and then another. Before long my sense of direction had disappeared altogether and I was obliged to place complete trust in my incomprehensible partner.

Unexpectedly, he would sometimes stop, turn off the engine and signal for me to dismount. Then he would creep to the top of a ridge, survey the scene ahead and declare 'Bono'. We would remount and roar away again. The first time this happened I failed to hang on tightly enough and as he sped away I tumbled off the machine backwards. My cries were drowned by the engine noise and my guide did not instantly notice my absence. He drove on for fully 200 yards down the hillside before he sensed something was drastically wrong. After the first few seconds, I had visions of Bruno reaching Cisterna without realizing his Very Important Passenger was missing.

Apart from bruises to my pride, I was uninjured by the fall and more importantly the radio seemed undamaged. Bruno soon returned and his look of concern changed into a huge grin which split his face like a slice of melon when he knew his precious cargo was unharmed. I remounted and clung tighter to my chuckling comrade as we set off once more, bouncing down the hillside in the general direction of Cisterna. For several minutes more we bumped along until Bruno slowed the machine to a stop. There was no sign of danger, but Bruno obviously knew we had to proceed cautiously. He explained as best he could that we were close to the main road linking Turin and Asti. With a combination of sign language and slow, carefully pronounced Italian — his dialect baffled me completely — Bruno made clear that convoys of enemy troops used the route constantly. There was no way to cross it without the risk of a patrol coming along at the wrong time. Fortunately I had one or two useful gadgets in my pack. Apart from a small quantity of explosives, which were to come in handy later, I also had a dozen sets of puncture spikes. These were a delightful invention for the guerrilla fighter. A triangular star of metal had a series of sharp points sticking out of it at three different angles. Dropped in the road they would blow the tyres of a vehicle no matter from which direction it came.

When Bruno and I saw that the main road was clear, we

took the opportunity to scatter the devices up and down a 200-yard section of the road near Villanova d'Asti. Then we crossed and headed once more for Cisterna. I figured that if any troop-carrying vehicles were looking for us, they would have to proceed on foot from that point. Bruno's wicked grin emerged again as we rode away from our tyre traps.

Our joy was short-lived, however. A few minutes later we rounded a bend on a quiet country road and scattered a German bicycle patrol. There was no time to decide what to do, because we were on to them before there was time to think. I am sure, on reflection, that this is what saved us. If we had seen them earlier and tried to stop, we would have been in all sorts of trouble, but, given no time to pause for thought, we just accelerated through them and away as they wobbled out of our path. They were so close I felt bodies brushing and bouncing off me as we roared through the group of twenty of them. Moments later I heard the familiar sound of guns firing and bullets zipping through the air all around me. Ricochets sparked off the stones in the ill-made road by my feet. Happily the safety of the next bend was not far away.

This unexpected encounter was both unnerving and decisive. We knew the chances were high that one of the cyclists would carry a radio with which he could report our position to his comrades. From this moment we threw caution to the wind.

I had imagined earlier that Bruno was travelling at top speed. I now knew differently as he stepped up the pace and we hurtled round corners and skidded over meadows. We also seemed to be taking a more direct route, ignoring the farm tracks and lanes in favour of fields and wooded hill-sides. Gaps in hedges were exploited to the full as Bruno gave a virtuoso performance on his rusty but trusty machine.

Perhaps the German bullets had sparked him into action, but I suspect otherwise. He was probably using discretionary caution earlier because of strict orders from Renato. Our brush with the enemy cyclists had given Bruno the chance he wanted to show off to me his amazing riding talents. A journey which had taken two days on foot with Captain

Keany took approximately 1½ hours as we returned by motor-bike. Bruno waved to the hillside guards as we pressed on to the castle at Cisterna.

I dismounted and told an anxious Partisan, 'I have some urgent news for Major Hope and Otello.' Bruno added some excited chatter and I was hustled in to the castle with the minimum of formality. My escort took me straight into a boardroom where the Major, Otello and other senior officers were poring over a map of the Langhe region. Instinctively I threw up a salute to Major Hope, stamped to attention and blurted out, 'I am sorry to report, sir, that Captain Keany has been killed.'

There were between sixteen and twenty officers in the room, but for five seconds you could have heard a pin drop. Then everybody started talking at once.

'*Povero Capitano e morte,*' the Italians explained to each other.

'*Poverino* (poor fellow)' was repeated over and over by the stunned Partisans, who had come to believe Keany's faith in his own immortality. Some men actually broke down and wept at the loss of the laughing Irishman we had all come to love.

VI

THE LONG ROAD TO CISTERNA

The death of Captain Keany was not only a sad loss for me on a personal level. During the weeks I had known him on such a constant and intimate basis, we had become close comrades despite the gap in rank. One of the most attractive features of membership of the S.O.E. was the fact that we all felt like equally important members of a team. But now Keany's untimely death had not only robbed me of a friend it had also wrecked my mission to Milan. I had been given merely the broad outline of the reason for our presence behind enemy lines. It was our job to help the Partisans to prevent the Germans from operating a scorched earth policy as they withdrew from Italy.

It was feared by Churchill and the War Cabinet that as soon as Hitler realized he would have to pull his troops out of Italy, he might try to wreck the country's economy. The Führer could choose to create a chaotic situation there in which the vacuum would be filled by the local Communists. This might then lead to a conflict between the Allied troops of Britain and America and the Italian Communists, which could, in turn, deflect Russia's attention from its relentless pressure westwards towards the heart of Germany.

All the while, the Nazis' development of an atomic bomb was making progress and we were in no doubt that, although the tide of the war was turning in our favour, it was by no means all over bar the shouting. Unless Germany was defeated quickly they might win the race to produce a war-winning weapon and Britain could become the target for the kind of devastation later wreaked on Hiroshima and Nagasaki.

So the job of the S.O.E. in northern Italy was to befriend the Partisans, supply them and help their disruption of Fascist activities. But we were also under instructions to try to persuade them to allow the Allies to liberate the major cities with the Partisans in a supporting role. The thinking behind this plan was that it would ensure that the Communists did not try to seize and hold power in Italy. Unfortunately there was no way these patriotic Partisans were going to be denied their hour of glory when the time came. Those of us living and fighting with them soon realized that nothing we could say would deprive them of that emotive and joyous occasion. Many of them had sacrificed everything they owned to live as outlaws, risking the lives of themselves and their families. What kept them going was the thought that one day soon they would return to their villages, towns and cities in triumph.

I had heard Keany, Roccia and Hope discussing the situation. They had come to the conclusion that, as the Partisans were intent on liberating their territory in person, our best plan was to give greatest support to the non-political Autonomous group and to the politically central Justice and Liberty Party. By helping them into Asti, Turin and Milan first, we could then use them to prevent any immediate seizure of power by the Communists before the Allied troops arrived.

Much of the political manoeuvring was way over my head at that time. All I knew was that Keany's sad death was in serious danger of ruining one of my last chances of making a name for myself before the war ended. By the time I had recovered from the shock of my Captain's death, I was starting to feel sorry for myself. I also felt anger that all my training, not only back in England, but later in North Africa, Sicily, Salerno and Anzio, might be wasted. It had been a long journey from the S.S. *Arundel Castle* on the River Clyde, Glasgow, in November, 1942, to the Cisterna Castle at Piedmont in March, 1945. As I went to sleep that night,

7 (Left): Settimo Maggiorino: "an accomplished mountaineer who seemed to know every blade of grass in Piedmont." (p.49)

8 (Right): Group Bombardier Jack Temple, "a handsome young volunteer from Texas". (p.125)

9 Major Mauri (second from left, in Alpine hat) with Partisans at the place where we crossed the River Tanaro (p.51)

10 Major Adrian Hope. "His corpse, still in uniform and draped with a Union Jack, lay in an open coffin overnight with a formal guard of honour." (p.153)

11 Corporal Shady Lane (p.159), 'Aldo', the author and Corporal Cormack in Turin.

I remember thinking: 'Surely I've not gone through all this for nothing.'

My thoughts strayed back to all that training at Pembroke and Chepstow, at Thetford and Catterick, at Chesterfield and Henley. And I remembered the amazing journey from Gourock to Algiers, the first time I had ever left my native shores. Thousands of troops were on board the *Arundel Castle* that night in November, 1942. It was a Union Castle passenger liner which had been commissioned as a troopship. Smaller boats ferried us out to this enormous vessel which was one of a convoy of twenty similar ships. We were escorted by an aircraft carrier and two destroyers as we set sail at daybreak.

German U-Boats had been taking a terrible toll of our shipping. By then we had lost perhaps half our merchant navy fleet to an enemy which lurked above, on, and, most menacingly, below the surface. On our second day at sea, however, it was not the evil forces of Hitler but the power-ful forces of nature which posed the greater threat to our voyage. We were heading for the middle of the Atlantic to avoid contact with the submarines which prowled the direct routes between Britain and the Mediterranean. Having succ-essfully escaped the attention of the enemy, we were attacked instead by the worst storms for fifty years.

Although the *Arundel Castle* was a passenger liner, I doubt the good ship would have attracted much in the way of cus-tom if they had crammed their clients into the accommo-dation with which we were provided. Our quarters com-prised a series of three-tier bunks into which forty-eight of us were packed like sardines. Safety boards were inserted at the sides of the bunks, but when the gales started men were falling down like leaves in autumn. The smell of vomit was overpowering and created further nausea. But it's an ill wind that blows nobody any good, and I reaped the benefit in an unexpected way.

As my memory serves me, a cockney called Drinkwater and I were the only men on board who were not seasick. I can offer no explanation for my welcome discovery of sea legs. It was just one of those things, and the bonus was a ready supply of extra rations from my shipmates. They were unable to hold down any food. Even the thought of it made them ill. So Drinkwater and I were given as much food as we could eat by our luckless comrades. I had not seen eggs for months, so I was able to indulge my passion for eating in general and for boiled eggs in particular. Drinkwater and I must have been the only two men on board who were disappointed when the storm eventually blew over and our shipmates regained their appetites.

We had not been told our destination, but somebody recognized the lights of Spain as we entered the Mediterranean. It did not take a military genius then to work out we were heading for Algiers to take part in the North African campaign. But, having survived the worst the weather could throw at us, our troubles were by no means over. One of our convoy, the troopship *Strathallen,* was torpedoed by a U-Boat. We heard they had suffered many casualties, although the ship itself managed to limp into port.

When we docked at Algiers, a group of fifty of us were told to march immediately to a signal station at Cap Matifou fifteen miles east of Algiers. Our party must have looked anything but a pretty sight as we tried to walk with parade-ground precision after our stormy journey. There had been no time to adjust to our land legs following a life on the ocean waves. So we must have looked a poor bunch as we marched and rolled towards our new billet – more like a gang of drunken sailors than an elite fighting unit.

My job at Cap Matifou was to send coded signals back to London reporting the progress of the North African campaign and messages from our agents in southern France, Italy, Corsica and Sardinia. The war was more than three years old and I was doing something useful for the first time. Working alongside me was another group of British S.O.E. men who were wearing American army uniforms. I never got to the bottom of this particular mystery, although it was explained to me vaguely that it was because they were cooperating with a Vichy French outfit. It seemed these French patriots looked more favourably on the Americans than the British, so S.O.E. decided to make them feel more comfortable about peaceful coexistence by dressing our men up as Yanks. This was not an overwhelming success because within a few days of my arrival an admiral named Darlan was shot and some Frenchmen from our unit were arrested.

If my recollection of these extraordinary events sounds slightly fragmented, confused or absurd, I can only plead that, to a 20-year-old private from Oldham, life certainly seemed fragmented, confused and absurd. The two officers in charge of us were a Squadron Leader Mallory and a Major Kay. At one stage Mallory disguised himself as an Arab and set off for Tunis on a secret mission. He was never seen alive again.

With this kind of eccentric behaviour going on all around me, I soon found the business of sending messages, albeit real ones at last, rather tedious. Like my colleagues I sought relief from the boredom in the bars of the town. One such escapade, in which I drank myself into semi-oblivion, nearly brought an ignominious end to my so far inglorious military career.

As I returned from a particularly heavy session with the boys, I had some kind of suicidal brainstorm which led me into the Officers' Mess. There I announced to all and sundry that in the opinion of Private Bill Pickering they were the least useful members of the British Army. This unsolicited view was expressed in rather colourful language, littered with obscene anatomical references, and earned me fourteen days in the glasshouse 'for abusing an officer while drunk'. But once again this crushing setback proved to be a blessing in disguise.

From the guardhouse, in the sober light of day, I wrote a cringing letter of apology to the commander, Colonel Dodds-Parker, in which I explained my frustration and eagerness for action. This did not lead to instant excitement and adventure, but it started a chain of events which were to lead me all the way to Cisterna.

First, I was posted at the end of my sentence to Club des Pins, some ten miles west of Algiers, where I was to help set up a main relay station back to London. This was given the cumbersome codename of Massingham Interservice Signals

Unit 6. Part of my duties were also to train American paratroopers from the Office of Strategic Services in radio-signalling techniques. They had come from Fort Benning in Georgia. The O.S.S. was their equivalent of S.O.E. and there were rumours that some of these swarthy American-Italian agents were Mafia hitmen on leave of absence from the Mob. I never found the courage to ask if these whispers had any truth in them.

Shortly after my posting, I received my first promotion. I became Lance-Corporal Pickering on the recommendation of a Corporal Smith, which was approved by a Captain Corbett. Ironically this was one of the captains I had insulted during my sozzled speech in the Officers' Mess. It somewhat restored my faith in the officer classes to realize that they bore no grudges.

More important than the promotion, however, was the fact that at the Club des Pins I met Major Malcolm Munthe, the in-field leader of the S.O.E. and a man who was to shape my destiny in many ways. It was he who told me about a heavy water plant which the Germans were building in Scandinavia. Munthe explained that if the Nazi experiments were successful, a single bomb would be able to devastate a city the size of London. Naturally I dismissed such a notion as the ramblings of a well-educated lunatic. But at least I had learned to hold my tongue and keep such thoughts to myself. As a result of this new-found diplomacy on my part, Munthe included me in his team when a hand-picked group of S.O.E. men landed in Sicily in the summer of 1943.

I arrived by Landing Ship Tank as back-up to Munthe's outfit. They had been on the island for a week and they were already establishing links with agents and anti-Fascists throughout Sicily.

Major Munthe was 6 feet tall, blond and in his mid-twenties. He was the son of Professor Axel Munthe, noted author of the best-seller *The Story of San Michele*. It was surprising, therefore, to discover that Munthe was hopeless at spelling. Despite his ancestry and public school education, the Major had to have childish errors corrected in his messages by Lance-Corporal Pickering from Oldham. I checked first to make sure his howlers were not some significant code and Munthe confessed he had always been the school dunce when it came to spelling.

He was a quiet, thoughtful man who was completely fearless. From time to time he would put forward absolutely madcap schemes to infiltrate the enemy lines. On one such occasion this involved getting Corporal Billy Beggs (with whom I had trained at Henley) to dress as a Sicilian peasant woman. Even Munthe finally recognized the folly of this particular scheme and abandoned it when the six-foot-tall Beggs clambered on to a donkey in traditional dark clothing with his size 10 boots dragging in the dust on either side of the startled animal.

Yet some of Munthe's wild ideas succeeded simply because of their breathtaking audacity. I nearly took part in one myself later when we planned to break out of our Anzio beachhead in a German ambulance.

Serving under Munthe were Captains Charles Mackintosh, Gilbert Randall, Dick Cooper and Max Salvadori, who at that time was known as Max Sylvester. Like Munthe, Captain Mackintosh was tall, fair and in his mid-twenties. He had worked for the Shell Oil Company in South America prior to the outbreak of war and he spoke both Italian and Spanish fluently. Mackintosh was unfailingly polite with a tremendous sense of humour. He and Captain Randall were the jokers in our pack. Randall was also quick to see the funny side of even the darkest moment. Nothing ever seemed to rattle this dark-haired soldier, who was also single and in his mid-twenties.

None of them had the military experience of Captain Cooper, who had an English father and an Italian mother. Cooper had been born in Baghdad, ran away from home and joined the French Foreign Legion as a teenager. Although of only medium height, he was a tough, hard-bitten character who had seen it all. By this time he was in his early forties and he was already fluent in Arabic, Turkish, French, Greek, Italian and Spanish.

Another member of our team was Flight Lieutenant Betts of the R.A.F. He had been a hotel manager in Sicily before the war and knew the geography of the island and some of its anti-Fascist inhabitants. This dapper former hotelier also spoke fluent Italian and French.

Leading the 'other ranks' was Sergeant Denis McDonnell, a big brawny Scotsman with a luxuriant moustache. McDonnell, whose home was on the shores of Loch Lomond, looked as if he would be more at ease in a kilt at the Braemar Highland Games tossing a caber. But nobody had the nerve to suggest such a thing. In any event we may not have understood his verbal reply to such a proposition because it was difficult to comprehend his thick accent without an interpreter.

Last but not least in this motley crew were my old Henley buddies, Corporals Billy Beggs and Harry Hargreaves, my fellow pillagers of the wine and brandy store.

Our group was well supplied with jeeps, communications equipment and personal weapons. I was assigned to work with Captains Mackintosh and Randall as their radio operator. This time it was my job to put the messages into code, so for the first time in the war I actually knew what was going on.

The Captains were assiduously gathering information from agents in the field as the Germans retreated before the Allied advance through Sicily. At first our billet was a tent in a field which we shared with a group of American radio operators. They had massive sophisticated transmitters and receivers supplied by generators which ran from trucks.

Despite their state-of-the-art technology, our American cousins were having tremendous difficulties getting through to their Algiers H.Q. They were amazed when I showed them my suitcase radio, pulled out a 50-foot length of wire, made a loop, fitted a stone in it and threw it into a nearby tree. They were even more astonished when I tuned in and immediately started receiving signals loud and clear from Algiers at a strength of QSA5. The Yanks, with all their heavyweight equipment, could only achieve a strength of QSA1 which was virtually unreadable. It made them green with envy when they saw my Mickey Mouse set getting maximum results. I hope I did not harm the spirit of cooperation between the American and British allies by looking too smug and self-satisfied by their discomfort.

After two days under canvas we moved to a top floor flat at 11, Via Maestranza, in Syracuse, which overlooked the ancient port. Captain Mackintosh left on a mission and Captain Randall and I were then joined by Sergeant Charlie Borg, a Maltese member of the S.O.E., and two Italian anti-Fascists named Babin and Vivanti.

Sergeant Borg had been a policeman in Malta before the war, but he had the appearance of a Chicago gangster. If Al Capone had needed a bodyguard he could have done a lot worse than this 6-foot-tall, overweight, menacing figure with a swarthy complexion and dark, curly hair, aged about 30. Definitely a good man to have on your side. As a bonus he spoke Italian, French, Spanish, Greek and Arabic.

Gianni Babin was a former professional boxer who had put on a few pounds since his middleweight days. His time in the ring had not damaged his ruggedly handsome looks, nor had he allowed being thumped for a living to change his jolly disposition. Babin was aged about 30, like his comrade Vivanti, although the latter was fair and chubby. They had been seconded to work with the S.O.E. because of their impeccable anti-Fascist records and their fluent Italian.

After two weeks in Syracuse a Dakota flew our party to Palermo, which was now occupied by American troops. We were the only non-Americans in the Sicilian capital (apart from the natives, of course), because the British army was building up its forces round the retreating Germans at Messina. We drew our rations from the American PX store, where we became firm friends with a Bilko-style figure called Captain Jones. I well remember the day when the good Captain gave us three pounds of oysters from General Mark Clark's supplies which he had left behind.

'All the other top brass are quarrelling about who should have these oysters,' said Captain Jones. 'Well I've decided to settle the argument by giving them all to you guys.'

We gratefully accepted this unexpected windfall and polished them off with relish at our latest billet, a flat at 45, Via Dante, Palermo. The Allied advance was gaining momentum by now and I seemed to be always one step behind the front line.

Before we could settle into our new home in Palermo, the British 8th Army had invaded Italy across the Straits of Messina and were pushing up the toe of the mainland. The S.O.E. had sent a unit to Salerno comprised of Munthe, Salvadori (still known as Sylvester), Mackintosh, Cooper, McDonnell, Beggs, Hargreaves and a Scots driver known as 'Jock' Fraser.

I left Sicily a week after the invasion with Captain Randall, Sergeant Borg, Babin and Vivanti. By this time the allied advance had already reached Naples so the five of us were able to drive a jeep on to the beach at Salerno at night after a pleasantly uneventful daylight crossing. We drove for some two hours to the Villa Salve in the Vomero district north of Naples, which was to be our new home for the next few months. The villa became the headquarters of No 1 Special Force in Italy. It provided a panoramic view across the Bay of Naples to Mount Vesuvius.

A few days after our arrival I watched in awe the breathtaking sight of Vesuvius erupting in all its power and glory. Grey smoke billowed upwards, illuminated by red flames as debris was hurled towards heaven by the supreme forces of nature. Scarlet streams of molten lava could be seen all night from our grandstand position 15 miles away.

Munthe was in charge of our outfit, although a middle-aged contessa who could be seen wandering the small courtyard surrounding the villa made it clear on occasions that we were only tenants on a short-term lease. She was obviously a reluctant hostess and looked down her nose at officers and other ranks without prejudice.

Apart from Munthe, Randall, Mackintosh, Cooper, McDonnell, Hargreaves, Beggs and Fraser, we were joined at the Villa Salve by Sergeant Frank Gee, who was in charge of administration. He was later to become a town councillor in Sale, near Manchester.

Our cook, Johnny Zivoli, was another staunch anti-Fascist who was housed separately in the villa with fellow countrymen Babin and Vivanti. The group also included a lieutenant who used to ply the lower ranks with drinks from his whisky ration and invite us to 'go for a spin' in his requisitioned brown Lancia. We were happy to accept his drinks, but there was something slightly effeminate in the lieutenant's manner which made us resist any desire for car rides. Our party was completed by a mechanic called Guiseppe whose 11-year-old son Pasquelino ran errands for us.

One of our regular visitors was Captain Michael Gubbins, son of Major-General Sir Colin Gubbins, the head of S.O.E. He was working as a transit agent, taking specialized agents into and out of northern Italy through the enemy lines. Gubbins was in his early twenties, tall, dark and handsome. He had been seconded from the Cameron Highlanders and was a young public-school educated gentleman who never displayed an ounce of snobbery or conceit over being the boss's son.

By the time we reached Naples the front line was only a few miles north of the city. General Mark Clark's 5th Army H.Q. had been set up at Caserta and our job was to run agents into and out of enemy-held territory. My specific task was to teach agents the art of radio transmission before they went on their missions. McDonnell, Beggs, Hargreaves and I sent and received coded messages via Algiers back to London. A War Office high-grade cipher book was used by Gee to code and decode the reports from and for our agents.

One of them, Adrian Gallegos, had already achieved a politically important coup for the S.O.E. Setting off by boat from Capri, Gallegos had slipped across to Sorrento where the Germans were holding the elderly Italian philosopher Benedetto Croce under unofficial house arrest.

Croce was a widely-respected anti-Fascist and the Nazis were afraid to upset Italian public opinion by arresting him openly. On the other hand they could not afford to allow him free speech, knowing he would undermine their position. So they compromised by keeping him a virtual prisoner in his own home — until Gallegos rescued him from under their noses.

I met Signor Croce at Villa Salve and was privileged to shake his hand. He was appalled to see the conditions of the poor citizens of Naples, who were suffering from a severe outbreak of typhus. The entire population of two million had to be deloused and all water supplies were boiled to control the spread of the disease.

Despite these precautions, I contracted a virulent form of dysentery in December, 1943. I spent five days in hospital and had been out less than 24 hours when I was readmitted with hepatitis. When I was released for the second time on 23 December I was warned that eating anything other than fish could cause a relapse. But, two days later, the sight of a traditional Christmas dinner was too much for a young lad of 20 a long way from home. So I tucked into the turkey with all the usual trimmings and extra rations of beer, with no ill effects.

Then we all took part in a sing-song round the gramophone, joining in an original German version of Lili Marlene. This was followed by a demonstration of hypnotism by the multi-talented Captain Cooper, who managed to put Hargreaves and myself into a trance. Apparently we were persuaded to do all manner of strange things while under hypnosis. Perhaps it is for the best that I do not know what they were.

The following day, Boxing Day, Hargreaves and I had hardly recovered from the trance and the extra beer ration when we were shipped by Motor Torpedo Boat to Ischia, an island in the Bay of Naples. The former Italian naval vessel, steered by Lieutenant Simpson-Jones (not the lieutenant in the brown Lancia, I hasten to add), averaged 35 knots and we made the morning crossing in half an hour.

By now the Allies had command of the seas and skies and we were in no danger. The land armies were gathering many miles away around the legendary monastery at Monte Cassino, and Ischia was a perfect jumping-off point for running agents to and from the west coast of Italy.

I had learned how to use plastic explosives in North Africa, where we would amuse ourselves by using short fuses and catching fish by lobbing the bombs into the water and then retrieving the unconscious creatures when they floated to the surface. My job at Ischia was to pass on to the agents my knowledge of explosives and radio transmission.

My pupils were particularly impressed with my angling technique, which led to a tasty snack of barbecued fish. Apart from the plastic explosive, which was like plasticine with tiny detonators stuck in it, we also used gun cotton explosive – small white bricks which could be wrapped round walls and bridge supports.

During our stay on the island, teaching explosives and transmission tips to the growing band of anti-Fascists who were joining our group, I lived in an old villa with Lieutenant Simpson-Jones, Hargreaves and the agent Gallegos, who had rescued Signor Croce.

Gallegos was a quiet, unassuming character in his mid-thirties. He had an indeterminate Mediterranean background, was of medium build and had dark hair and deep-set eyes. His job with S.O.E. was mainly to select dropping points and to accompany agents to and from their missions. As I taught a shorthand form of Morse code at the agents' 'school' on Ischia, Lieutenant Simpson-Jones and Gallegos would set sail with my graduated pupils in the M.T.B.

They would always cast off as soon as darkness fell and usually Simpson-Jones returned before dawn with a different agent on board. From time to time Captain Cooper would come across to the island. Ostensibly he was there to give last-minute instructions to his departing agents, although I suspect he was also checking that the notorious Pickering was behaving himself. By this time I had reached the dizzy heights of Corporal, but my respect for authority had not improved noticeably.

I was allowed to beg a free ride on the M.T.B. on a couple of occasions when we were taking out our scouts. It was during one such expedition that the Lieutenant spent a great deal of time studying a particularly long stretch of beach and made detailed notes.

'Where's that?' I inquired.

'It's a place called Anzio,' he replied.

We spent two and a half weeks on Ischia, during which time more than a dozen agents were sent ashore, usually by black rubber dinghy. One of the unlucky ones was Gianni Babin, the happy-go-lucky pro boxer.

Word came back to us that Babin had been caught by the Germans, staked out on the beach and run over by a tank. Whatever the truth of that rumour, certainly Babin was never seen alive by us again.

When Simpson-Jones took Hargreaves and I back to the mainland, I was told to report to Major Munthe at the Villa Salve. There I was shepherded into a room with Captains Gubbins and Salvadori and four newcomers. One was a driver from Liverpool known as 'Scouser' Mulvey – a small, wiry fellow of 24. Mulvey was a great one for the dry, witty remark, like so many Merseysiders. But at times of excitement he could develop an alarming stammer – the last thing you needed in an emergency.

The second was a namesake of mine who had risen rather higher in the ranks but not off the ground. Major Pickering was a tiny chap, perhaps 5 feet 3 inches tall. He was aged around 30 and slightly timid, but he had been brought up in Alsace-Lorraine, spoke fluent German and had been borrowed from the S.O.E.'s German section.

The third stranger in our midst was an elderly gent, well into his fifties, named Alberto Tarchiani. He was tall, silver-haired and bespectacled. Signor Tarchiani had served a prison sentence for his anti-Fascist beliefs and he was accompanying us to rally the support of kindred spirits on our mission. This distinguished-looking politician was later to become the Italian Ambassador to Washington at the end of the war.

He was accompanied by another Italian called John Saville, who had been educated in England. Saville was something of a mystery man to me. He had served with the Royal Tank Regiment but his greatest concern seemed to be the location of his missing fiancée in Rome. I later learned his real name was Luigi Savilli, who had an Italian father and a British mother.

Major Munthe addressed us all at the meeting in the Villa Salve on 21 January, 1944.

'Gentlemen,' he announced. 'It has been decided that a beachhead is to be formed at Anzio in two days' time. From there we will head for Rome. It is our honour and privilege to be leading the way.'

The Major went on to tell each man his general duties in the plan to create a pincer movement which would entrap the German armies defending Monte Cassino.

I had been chosen as the group's radio operator. In football parlance I was 'over the moon'. Here was real excitement, an adventure at last.

It was not the done thing to register excitement. Soldiers always pretended to take everything the world could throw at them in their stride. So it was with our enthusiastic band. All of us assumed a matter-of-fact air about the operation ahead of us, although I suspect we were all on a high of adrenalin.

We left Naples on the night of 22 January in a Landing Ship Tank. No other vessel was in sight as the Greek captain steered us towards our destination, but when we arrived at dawn the following morning, a veritable armada of ships was lined up waiting to head for shore.

Unfortunately the weather was too rough for craft like ours which had to land on the beach. Conditions had been kinder 24 hours earlier when the main force arrived unopposed and formed a beachhead. By now those troops – two divisions of Americans, one division of British and two battalions of American Rangers – had dug themselves in to await the enemy's counterattack.

The weather had now taken a turn for the worse with overcast skies and blustery winds. We had the frustrating job of lying in a choppy sea with twenty or thirty other ships which were queueing up to land as soon as the situation improved. I was thankful once again that seasickness was not a problem for me, but some of my comrades were less fortunate. We rocked and rolled, pitched and tossed until just before dusk when a new threat materialized to take our minds off the sea conditions – an enemy air attack.

We were like sitting ducks when the Luftwaffe came over to make what proved to be one of their last big efforts of the war. As the Messerschmitt fighters and Focke-Wolf fighter-bombers roared into action, we were ordered to our cabins by the ship's captain. But when one of his crew came along to batten down the hatches of our room, Mulvey and I were of the same opinion.

'Blow that for a game,' stammered Mulvey (or words to that effect).

Without further ado we unbattened the hatches and went on deck. The idea of being hit while trapped in a cabin did not appeal to us at all. The risk of being either burned alive by the fuel on board or sent to Davy Jones's Locker in a steel airtight tomb seemed equally appalling. At least on deck we could see what was happening.

So Mulvey and I crouched behind the ventilation shafts and surveyed the scene. One of our cruisers was belching black smoke half a mile away and other vessels were taking hits all around us. In addition to the aerial bombardment, we were also taking a pounding from a heavy gun which became known as 'Anzio Annie'. It was somewhere in the Alban Hills which surround Rome and which command a dominating view of the Anzio shoreline.

But the Axis troops were not having things all their own way. Our larger ships were returning the fire both on to the German artillery and the Luftwaffe. The air was thick with the smell of smoke and cordite. The noise was deafening. Apart from the background thud of the heavy Bofors guns there was the higher-pitched whine of the Oerlikons firing tracer shells at the planes. Added to all this was the intermittent roar of the aircraft engines as they flew their low-level sorties.

I saw eight enemy planes out of an estimated sixty hit by the ships' guns. One just exploded in mid-air, presumably the victim of a heavy-duty shell, and appeared to disintegrate completely. The remainder were hit by tracer shells and trailed black smoke as they tried to limp home.

While Mulvey and I were watching this awesome display of firepower meteing out death and destruction on a massive scale all around us, we were playing a high-stakes game of hide-and-seek with the Luftwaffe behind the ventilation shafts. As the planes made their raids from different directions we would hop round behind the shafts to dodge the withering fire. It proved a simple, but effective, technique — and we certainly felt safer than our officer comrades, locked in their cabins.

The air raids seemed to go on for an eternity, but must have lasted some 15 minutes. When the close-quarter firing ended and we realized that the remaining planes were heading home, comparative silence fell over the area. The dull thuds of Anzio Annie could still be heard, yet it was as peaceful as a Sunday School outing in contrast to the chaotic cacophony moments earlier.

One of our larger ships was ablaze from stem to stern in the distance and three others had taken serious hits. As we studied the scene with darkness falling, I prayed the planes would not return again at dawn. I was not looking forward to a repeat performance, especially as our L.S.T. was unarmed. We may have enjoyed the sport of it more if we had been able to shoot back. In the event my prayers were answered. The weather improved. The sea calmed and at dawn the next day we landed at Anzio.

Major Munthe drove one jeep containing Gubbins, Major Pickering and Saville. Mulvey took the wheel of another in which Salvadori, Tarchiani and myself were the passengers. We followed Munthe as he drove up the coast road north of Anzio.

Artillery and mortar shells were falling all over the place as we drove along the occasionally cratered road. I could see no pattern to the shelling. The enemy seemed to be sending their stuff in our general direction and the Allies were doing the same back.

Munthe overshot our front line and headed for a farmhouse in No-Man's-Land. Mulvey followed. We dashed indoors and I reported our position from the front room. By now the Germans seemed to be concentrating their fire on us, but this failed to impress Munthe. He strolled round the farmyard wearing his green Gordon Highlanders kilt and seemed completely oblivious to the shells which were raining down all around him. Captain Gubbins, in the predominantly red tartan of the Cameron Highlanders, was equally unmoved by the mayhem.

Perhaps it is the public school upbringing which prevents an English gentleman from flinching in the face of the enemy. But I did not share their enthusiasm for the job in hand when Munthe urged, 'Come along now, Pickering. There must be a frying pan lying around somewhere.'

I could not believe this was happening to me. We were risking life and limb for a cooked breakfast. Munthe did not appear to recognize the danger. As we wandered in and out of the farm buildings, he pointed to a group of Allied soldiers crawling on their bellies along the trench lines behind us.

'What on earth are they doing?' he asked with genuine incredulity.

In my younger days I might have been inclined to reply, 'Acting sensibly, unlike us,' but I held my tongue. On this occasion fortune favoured the brave and we led charmed lives. But we never did find that elusive frying pan.

Salvadori had been taken ill during the sea journey. At first we had thought he was just suffering from mal-de-mer, but it was now clear that his condition was more serious. He had to take to a bed with jaundice that night.

The following morning, with salvoes from 88-millimetre shells and airbursts falling like confetti, we decided to pull out. Munthe and the other senior officers had taken Tarchiani and Saville in both jeeps to look for a safer billet. But it was no longer safe for them to come back to us or for us to wait for their return. There was nothing for it but to make a dash for it back to our front line 200 yards away.

The Germans were just 400 yards away from us when we started our zig-zag sprint. I was concerned that Salvadori might be too weak to run.

'Don't worry,' he said with an unconvincing smile. 'When they start shooting at me I'll be able to run all right.'

And so we set off together, jinking from side to side at irregular intervals to make life difficult for any marksmen. We had covered perhaps half the distance before the Germans responded. Then we heard the sound of their machine guns. Time seemed to stand still as bullets zipped all around us, whistling past our ears and exploding in the muddy field round our boots. I felt as though I was in a slow-motion film.

Despite the weight of my suitcase radio transmitter I imagine it took us less than 20 seconds to cover that final 100 yards under fire. Salvadori was as good as his word, temporarily shrugging off the energy-sapping effects of his jaundice.

For the last few yards I could hear the cheering of the soldiers from the Loyal North Lancashire Regiment who had been watching our deadly race from the comparative safety of the trenches. Simultaneously we leapt into three separate slit trenches which had been dug side by side ahead of the forward positions.

We barely had time to regain our breath when the German mortars started to find our range. In between their salvoes we heard the cries of our comrades urging us to get out. I saw two brown wooden crosses marking makeshift graves by the side of my trench and later learned that two men had been killed there the day before. I needed no further encouragement. We scrambled out of our short-lived refuges and sprinted another 100 yards to a sunken road below the enemy firing line.

This final effort had taken the last reserves of strength away from Salvadori. We were all exhausted, but it was obvious that our officer comrade needed medical attention. As we sat on our haunches panting, we noticed a line of a dozen British tanks hiding along the sunken road. I was told they were waiting for the overcast skies to clear so we could receive some air support from the high-altitude Flying Fortress bombers to cover the thrust forward from Anzio.

Just before lunchtime Munthe, Gubbins, Major Pickering, Tarchiani and Saville found us. The five of them helped the yellow-faced Salvadori into one jeep and told Mulvey and I to head to the NAAFI for rations. Munthe gave me a chit for the supplies and wished me good luck. He told me he planned to set up headquarters at the nearby Torre St Lorenzo and asked us to bring the rations back to him there. Munthe said he would take care of Salvadori's evacuation.

Mulvey and I decided to continue eastwards inland and then head south to the NAAFI some three miles north of Anzio. We judged it would be quicker than heading west for the coast road, going back to Anzio and then heading north for the supplies. This was not the smartest decision we ever made!

As soon as we drove past the tanks the road started to climb and the hedgerow shrank. We were in full view of the German front line who decided to use us for target practice. Within seconds all manner of shells and bullets were exploding and fizzing around us. Mulvey drove like an inspired demon, quickly reaching the maximum speed of 55 m.p.h. I clung grimly to the bar in front of me as we bounced over bomb craters, swerving to avoid the larger ones and ignoring the smaller potholes. Occasionally he would misjudge the size of the indentations and I felt as though all my fillings were likely to shake loose. I could not make up my mind whether I was more scared of the bombs and bullets or of Mulvey's driving. We ran the gauntlet for a full mile and then turned sharp right on two wheels. At this corner we had seen groups of British artillery returning the German fire. But as we reached it, the Allies took a direct hit from an enemy shell. I saw bodies flying high in the air among the smoke and debris as Mulvey regained control of the vehicle and sped on towards the NAAFI.

The intense shelling died down as we got further away from the German front line. Yet even after three miles, when we reached the stores, sporadic gunfire could be heard and the occasional explosion would keep everyone on his toes and his nerve-edges.

Our chit from Munthe was for 'compo' rations. These were white wooden boxes with the word 'compo' − short for composition − stencilled in black paint. They were supposed to contain enough supplies to feed ten men for one day. Mulvey and I collected six boxes. They were all identical. Imagination and variety were not the strong points of the purveyors of food and drink to the British Army. Each box contained tins of Irish stew, which were called Maconochies, tins of baked beans, Cheddar cheese, rice pudding, jam and margarine, powdered tea, sugar and milk, packets of dry, hard biscuits, a cylindrical packet of 50 Players' cigarettes, a tin opener and some matches.

The Americans were similarly fed up with their unvaried

supplies, which they called K Rations. We would swop our hard biscuits for their soft ones and change half the tins of Maconochies for their tins of corned beef hash. For fourteen days we saw no bread at Anzio.

Discretion being the better part of valour, we took the longer, more peaceful route back into Anzio and along the coast road before heading for the Tower of St Lorenzo. It was a four-storey brown brick building from which we could see for miles in every direction.

Munthe and the others had arranged for Salvadori to have hospital treatment back in Naples and they had settled in a barn 50 yards from the tower. A shell had virtually removed one of the walls and on bad days the wind fairly whistled through the gap, but we made the best of our new home as Munthe and Gubbins plotted our route to Rome.

Tarchiani and Saville usually stayed with Mulvey and I, while Munthe, Gubbins and Pickering probed for a weakness in the enemy line. I was sending regular coded reports back to base and we had been at Anzio for a week when Munthe told us his plan.

'We are going to drive through the enemy lines in an ambulance wearing German uniforms,' he announced.

'He's finally flipped,' I thought. But I continued to listen eagerly as he revealed his master strategy for reaching Rome to organize, supply and coordinate the Partisan resistance groups.

Munthe's idea was to convert one of our ambulances with a respray and to find some dead Germans from whom he could 'borrow' uniforms. He was liaising with an American infantry captain from the 34th Oklahoma Division who knew just where we could find some suitable bodies.

His men had surprised a German patrol in No-Man's-Land the previous night and the Captain offered to escort us to the spot where they had fallen. I was chosen to accompany Munthe and Gubbins, alias Burke and Hare, on their macabre mission.

The American Captain and a section of a dozen men led us stealthily to the bodies at midnight. The Americans took up covering positions and I was told to wait with them while

Munthe and Gubbins crawled over to the dead Germans a few yards away. I could just see their contorted, sprawled bodies from where I crouched. It looked as though they had been cut down by a surprise burst of American machine gun fire.

After a few minutes my two officers returned, each carrying two German jackets and two steel helmets.

'We're in business,' whispered Gubbins. 'There aren't enough for all of us, but enough to put on a show to fool Gerry.'

'They're both as mad as each other,' I thought.

The following day Munthe outlined his plan in greater detail. As soon as we had acquired and 'doctored' an ambulance, we would drive it through the enemy lines to Rome. There we would link up with anti-Fascist groups and coordinate their resistance. Because of our delay in breaking out of Anzio, the Gestapo were carrying out bloody reprisals against Italians who had started diversionary attacks at the time of the Allied landings. Many had been arrested, tortured and shot. As a result our intelligence network had been broken and it was vital we get through before it disintegrated completely.

Major Pickering was to don one of the looted uniforms and drive the ambulance because he spoke fluent German. Munthe and I were to share the front seat with him, also in uniform, because we had blond hair and were the most Germanic-looking of our group. Gubbins was to have the fourth uniform in the back of the ambulance, where Tarchiani and Saville were to lie under blankets pretending to be wounded. I cursed my luck for having fair hair and blue eyes. But the more I thought about this crazy-sounding scheme, the more I realized that it was audacious enough to work. None of the thousands of Germans we would have to pass in our ambulance would imagine that anyone in his right mind would attempt such a cheeky venture – and that could be our trump card.

A major hurdle to be cleared was the fact that the front line was becoming increasingly static. Munthe's scheme needed a fluid fighting line which he could infiltrate with his ambulance. Unfortunately the Germans, having held up our advance at Monte Cassino, were now collecting fresh forces on top of the Alban Hills with which to mount a counterattack. They had their own plans, which were to drive the British and American contingents off Anzio and into the sea.

At the beginning of February an Italian reached our lines from Rome. This was the break Munthe was looking for, and when he received a message that this man would show us the route back again, his joy knew no bounds. He and Gubbins set off to meet him in a cave near the front line where he was being fed and watered by some members of the Irish Guards. Munthe and Gubbins decided to meet this Italian and test the feasibility of the route before risking the entire complement of the team.

Munthe told me later what happened when he and Gubbins accidentally ventured beyond our front line to reach the cave. They crept along a ditch at the side of a road which led to a building known as 'The Factory'. It was in fact a bell tower which resembled a factory chimney. The road alongside the ditch where Munthe and Gubbins were inching their way led to a roundabout with a 12-foot-high cross in the middle.

As they made their way towards it, the two British officers brushed past a large broken branch which fell to one side and nearly made those imperturbable characters scream with fright. Leaning against the branch with his feet in the trench was a German soldier! His eyes were wide open and his mouth was set in a grin, but his face beneath the helmet was the colour of wax. They guessed he had been dead for some 24 hours.

As Munthe and Gubbins ran from the ditch towards the cross, their worst fears were realized. A machine gun opened up from The Factory at Aprilia. Unknown to them, the Allied line had fallen back temporarily. Their route to the cave was now in German hands.

It would have taken three or four minutes to cross the roundabout and reach the cave, exposed to fire almost every second of the way. Munthe immediately shouted 'Slit trench' as the enemy mortars opened up on them as well. The nearest contained the dead German so Munthe and Gubbins leapt into the one behind it five yards away. The mortars started to creep ever closer as their operators found the range. Munthe told me that Gubbins started to sing defiantly. He chose his favourite, the song he had sung on Christmas Day six weeks earlier on the night Hargreaves and I were hypnotized by Captain Cooper.

With the 'moaning minnies' falling all around them, Gubbins gave a stout rendition of 'Abdul the Bulbul'. Munthe described the sight of the mortars landing as being like invisible mushrooms popping up and sending showers of earth upon them in their trench. One shell fell into the next trench, hurling the dead soldier and his broken branch high into the air. Fittingly, Michael Gubbins had just sung the words, 'But of all the most reckless of life and of limb was Abdul the Bulbul Ameer' when he was killed.

Munthe told me how he heard the whine of the mortar as it came down to the left of them, where Gubbins was crouching forward. The Major shut his eyes and a tremendous thud filled the trench. He thought he was dead. Munthe felt a violent pain against his chest and highlights of his life flashed before him.

When he opened his eyes again, Gubbins was lying on his back with his eyes wide open, but his helmet was missing and his body was coloured crimson. Munthe saw blood all over his own body too.

The Major remembered trying to drag Gubbins out of the trench, by now oblivious to the mortar attack. But he had little recollection of the two stretcher-bearers who had seen him staggering down the road and who were hit themselves as they carried him to safety.

He told me of Gubbins' fate when I visited him in a dark brown hospital tent at Anzio a few days later. He was swathed in bandages round his head and chest where shrapnel had embedded itself. One piece had struck his chest and doctors told him that a photograph of his girlfriend in his breast pocket had probably saved his life. Another piece of the mortar bomb had implanted itself in the left side of his skull, threatening the sight of the eye. For Major Malcolm Munthe the war was over.

It had been Major Pickering who had brought news of Gubbins' death and Munthe's grave injury to us at the barn next to the Torre St Lorenzo. It was my painful duty to send the message via Naples back to London informing the head of S.O.E., Major-General Sir Colin Gubbins, that his brave son had died in action. He had been one of the kindest, most courageous young men I had met and my eyes filled with tears as I sent my coded despatch. Gubbins was buried in a makeshift grave at the spot where he was killed, but that grave was destroyed by subsequent shelling.

As I talked to Munthe in the field hospital, shells were dropping all over Anzio as the German counter-offensive reached its peak. Anzio Annie, also known as Whistling Willie, had wreaked havoc upon our beachhead. Nowhere was safe from danger.

At one stage an American nurse preparing to dress Munthe's wounds at the side of his bed was killed by a piece of shrapnel which pierced the tent. I was never more relieved than when the order came through to abandon the plan to reach Rome and get back to Naples.

So on the night of 12 February, Pickering, Tarchiani, Saville, Mulvey and I boarded an L.S.T. to head back to Naples. By this time elements from ten German divisions had surrounded Anzio and our shipping was taking a terrible pounding as it tried to bring in supplies and evacuate the wounded.

But we were unscathed at dawn the following morning when we saw the welcome sight of the harbour at Naples. I had been longing for a touch of excitement and adventure. But after three weeks in the hell of Anzio I had had a bellyful of action. It had given me a real fright and I thought I would never want to go near a battleground again. After waiting hungrily for more than three years for a taste of real fighting, I was more than happy to be out of range again. At that time I could never contemplate wanting to return to the front line, never mind parachute behind it into enemy territory!

After the carnage at Anzio I was relieved initially to spend a week at the Villa Salve sending reports via Algiers. Then I was informed that I had been promoted to sergeant and was being transferred to Monopoli, where I would be in charge of the signal office under Captain Derrick Scott-Job. This suited me fine. The further I moved away from the front line, the longer it would take me to get back again. My job would be to train ex-Italian Army radio operators who had switched sides to send and receive messages at the top S.O.E. speed.

Captain Scott-Job was a decent boss. He was a studious-looking type, aged about 24, with dark hair and horn-rimmed spectacles. But his calm and easy-going manner changed dramatically one day when I ignored one of his directives. I had not bothered to write down the frequencies with which my agents were sending signals. Because of the arrogance of youth I thought I knew better than the Captain and could keep the wavelengths in my head. But I was wrong. And when two of our radio operators found themselves trying to transmit on the same frequency at the same time, Scott-Job went purple with rage. He gave me the biggest dressing-down of my life; one which I had thoroughly deserved.

For four months I was in charge of the signals office at Monopoli. By the end of that time I was becoming bored and restless to be back in the fray. Time had obviously healed the painful memories of my Anzio experiences and I was champing at the bit once more. My request for active service was approved and I was sent for full training at the 'battle school' in San Vito, near Monopoli. We were toughened up by learning to sleep under the stars and to conjure up a five-course meal from a hedgerow. We were taught the art of silent killing, with commando knife, rope or bare hands. Our knowledge of weapons and explosives was honed, and we learned how to navigate at night. To put the theory into practice we would occasionally be dropped 100 miles from our base in the wild hills of Calabria without money. We were expected to use our initiative to make our way back again as quickly as possible.

Part of this training took me north of Rome, which had by then been liberated, where we were taught skiing and mountaineering. By the time I was moved to Cecina, near Leghorn, for the start of Operation Chariton, I was like a coiled spring again.

The horrors of Anzio were just a distant memory and I was itching to be on my way. But it seemed that, after going so far, the fates had conspired to frustrate me once more. All my training, all the dangers I had faced and all the time spent away from home looked like counting for nothing because of Keany's tragic death.

I was still feeling sorry for myself when I awoke in the castle of Cisterna the following morning. Then, to make matters worse, I learned that I had just missed one of the most spectacular against-the-odds victories of the war.

VII

THE BATTLE

The Partisans operating around Cisterna had been aware throughout that long hard winter that their increasing strength and activity was bound to attract reprisals from the Italian Fascists and Nazi occupiers. Intelligence reports confirmed that plans were being made to carry out a full-blooded and merciless attack on their stronghold as soon as the winter snows had disappeared.

Their commander, Otello – the codename by which Colonel Toselli was called with both reverence and affection – had been plotting his own tactics for a counterattack even before Keany and I set off on our ill-fated mission.

The winter of 1944-45 had been as bitterly cold as any local residents could remember. Consequently the deep snows and treacherous conditions had delayed the Fascist onslaught. But Toselli and his troops were under no illusions. As soon as spring had sprung, the enemy had been instructed to crush the bandits of Cisterna once and for all. Their orders were to storm the castle in a surprise attack and take it by sheer weight of numbers and superior arms.

Unknown to the Fascists of the Brigata Nera and the R.A.P., a particularly nasty bunch of anti-Partisans, our night-time drops during the winter had ensured that Otello and his band would not be at such a great disadvantage in the weaponry department. The S.O.E. had systematically supplied the Partisans with all they could handle in terms of guns, grenades, ammo and explosives.

Nevertheless they had to suffer anxious moments as the barren fruit, mulberry and chestnut trees of the region started to sprout its annual greenery at the end of February and beginning of March. As the snow retreated and the foliage grew, the smoke of fires could be seen in the distance. This was the all-too-familiar harbinger of approaching Fascists, as suspected Partisan sympathizers had their homes razed to the ground in punishment.

Major Hope told me the morning after Keany's death how the approaching Fascists had played an unnerving game of cat and mouse as they approached Cisterna. What the hundreds of men from the Brigata Nera never realized was that Otello had cast them in the parts of mice! Even so, it had taken an extraordinary piece of luck to save the day for the Autonomous Partisans.

Hope told me how, on the morning of 6 March, the bandits of Cisterna were sleeping soundly, safe in the knowledge that their sentries were guarding all approaches to the hilltop fortress. They would not have slept so well if they had known that several platoons of Fascist soldiers had slipped silently past the guards and started to climb a hillside leading to the tiny village of Valzeglio, less than a mile from the 11th Century castle.

If the Italian soldiers had reached the ridge they would have had little difficulty in achieving their objective and overwhelming the sleeping Partisans of Cisterna. But, at the vital moment, fate played its usual crucial role.

The French girlfriend of a Partisan named Aceto Ezio had been experiencing a troubled night in one of the cottages. She was suffering from agonizing stomach cramps and at 4 o'clock she could stand the pain no longer. She got out of bed and walked over to a window to study the stars as the change of position brought relief to her cramps. As the mademoiselle gazed sleepily out of the window, a movement caught her attention. She looked down the hillside and realized she had not been imagining things. A group of Fascist soldiers were making their way stealthily up the hillside and were only 200 yards from the ridge. The French heroine of the hour immediately roused her boyfriend,

Aceto, who grabbed his sub-machine gun from the wall where it was propped beside his bed ready for instant use. He took one look out of the window and knew there was no time to lose.

Aceto decided that the best way to warn his comrades without alerting the Fascists too soon of their peril was by opening fire. He took up a vantage point behind a wall where he had a perfect view of the enemy. Then he poured a withering volley of fire into their leading men.

'The Fascists had their hands full with climbing and were unable to return the fire at first,' Hope explained. 'By the time they had managed to find suitable positions, the rest of us were wide awake and running to support Aceto.'

For several minutes the Partisans poured bullets in the direction of the cowering soldiers. Then they started lobbing grenades at the men of the Brigata Nera. It was no contest. With their height advantage, the Partisans could hurl their grenades hundreds of yards downhill into the enemy positions where they wreaked a bloody toll of death and injury. For the Fascists to respond would have been the military equivalent of spitting into the wind.

The one-sided bloodshed went on for some thirty minutes until Otello advised his men to conserve their ammunition and to shoot only when they could identify a specific target. This reduction in the Partisans' firepower obviously created a false impression in the mind of the leader of the attackers.

Using a megaphone, he shouted during a lull in the fighting, 'Give yourselves up. You are completely surrounded. Your position is hopeless.'

Surrender was never on anyone's mind. The Fascists had embarked on a three-pronged attack with a 500-strong force approaching from Valmellana in the north, a similar number from Canale in the south, and several hundred more from San Damiano in the east. They were supported by three tanks, three armoured cars, two artillery guns, mortars, heavy and light machine guns. But now they were the victims of the near success of their surprise attack. Because a large contingent of their soldiers had come so close to the ridge, the distant artillery could not provide them with covering fire.

Otello realized that, although he had only 200 men against a force of more than a thousand, he was still holding the whip hand. He was also aware that unconditional surrender to the Fascists would quite probably result in his men being shot. From the ramparts of the ancient castle, he yelled a defiant message which may well have been an echo of similar taunts from mediaeval knights over the centuries.

'If you want us, you'll have to come and get us,' he roared. And he instructed his men to give the enemy a taste of what they could expect.

At the given signal the Partisans gave an awesome display of firepower as they raked the hillside below them with bullets and sent down a veritable orchard of pineapple grenades.

Hope told me, 'It was a tremendous tactical ploy by Otello. The easing up on firing had obviously given false hopes to the attackers. Their leaders had told them the Partisans were clearly running out of ammo. So when Otello told us to let rip, the Fascists knew they were facing an uphill struggle in every sense of the word. It was also a tremendous boost to the morale of our lot to know we had the upper hand and were on top of the situation.'

The deafening fusillade continued for a minute. Then Otello showed his expertise at close-quarter fighting. It was important that the men of the Brigata Nera should not be allowed to detach themselves from high on the hillside in close proximity to the castle's defenders.

Otello knew that, if they could create a No-Man's-Land situation, the Brigata Nera commanders would opt for the less hazardous procedure of long-range strikes with their artillery. So, like a boxer who keeps his opponent locked in a clinch, Otello manoeuvred his own and the enemy troops to his best advantage. Using his expert knowledge of the buildings and terrain, he sent small patrols of Partisans down the hillside to cut off the retreat of the leading Fascist soldiers. They were soon pinned down with fire from the front, side and rear.

Hope told me, 'This prevented the Republicans from using

long-range weapons in case they killed their own men. But Otello was crafty to the ultimate degree. He gave out orders that although he wanted the leading group of Fascists pinned down, he didn't want them slaughted. They were more valuable to him alive. He sent more Partisan patrols down the hillside beyond the advance group of Brigata Nera to wait patiently for the next wave who came to rescue their comrades. Otello knew they were bound to try to move forward to provide covering fire while they extricated the wounded. So the Partisans waited and watched as the Fascist reinforcements moved forward. They allowed the unsuspecting soldiers to advance up the hillside until they had them covered from both flanks and rear. Then they opened fire again. From the castle we had a perfect view of what was happening. It was like being in the Royal Box at the F.A. Cup Final. The Fascist soldiers had climbed into a classic trap. To use an Italian phrase, they had walked into the jaws of the wolf. The discipline of the Partisans was amazing. First one side would fire while their comrades took cover. The Fascists barely had time to pause for breath when they would come under a hail of bullets from the other side. Now Otello had more of his enemy pinned down in his trap. And still the Brigata Nera couldn't use its heavy guns.'

While the firing was at its height, my one-time guide Settimo Maggiorini was despatched to give urgent orders to Gino, who was in charge of a group of some sixty Partisans at St Luigi da Monta D'Albo. Otello was confident that the Fascist commander's claim to have Cisterna surrounded was a bluff. Nevertheless it must have taken considerable courage for Settimo to head off unarmed through the enemy lines on his red Gerbi bicycle.

Settimo, the craggy ex-Alpini Regiment soldier, had joined the Autonomous Partisans of Otello on 1 October, 1943, shortly after their formation. He and four others had been captured by the Fascists the following summer when a Republican spy led them into an ambush. The five of them had been taken into the local garrison at Canale where they overheard a German and an Austrian arguing about whether to shoot them immediately or interrogate them first. Fortunately the more humane Austrian's argument had won the day, and while the betrayed quintet waited to be tortured, the local Partisans were tipped off about their fate. Before its German patrol could return to the garrison, a lorry-load of twenty Partisans attacked the building, shot the Nazi guards and freed their prisoners.

Thereafter, Settimo became a familiar figure among the Partisans as he rode his red bike through the village streets around Cisterna wearing a distinctive white beret. Settimo was almost always unarmed and he had a rare talent for looking completely innocent if he was ever stopped by German or Italian Fascist patrols.

So it was with a degree of confidence that Otello sent Settimo pedalling away in the direction of Gino with instructions for him to attack the enemy from the rear. Towards the end of the first day of the Battle for Cisterna, the Fascist troops were at a pretty low ebb. They had lost some 200 men, achieved none of their objectives and had a large group of their soldiers unable to move safely in any direction. They must have thought things could only get better on the second day. But they were wrong!

Some of the braver Fascists pinned down on the hillside had managed to move back under cover of darkness to their comrades in the rearguard. For a short while they must have felt relieved to be out of immediate danger. That feeling did not last long.

As dawn broke, Gino and his men started attacking the main Brigata Nera force from the rear. They had also used the blanket of the night to move into position. And they knew the territory intimately.

Meanwhile Hope had led another group of Cisterna-based bandits into a dominating position overlooking the Fascists' right flank. He described to me what happened as the spring sunshine trickled over the hillside and spilled into the valley below.

'The Brigata Nera were resting when sniper fire took out two of their sentries,' he told me. 'This caused instant panic. Nobody seemed to know who was in charge and junior officers were bellowing out conflicting orders. As some men instinctively ran towards their fallen colleagues, other snipers picked them off. The Fascists didn't know which way to turn. As fast as they identified the danger from one sniper, another would open up from somewhere else.

'Blue shirts were turning red in front of us as the small force from St Luigi took its toll. Just as the Republicans had managed to restore some sort of order and found refuge from Gino's snipers, we opened up with a light machine gun.

'It's no great feat to shoot men in the back, but all's fair in love and war, and these men would have shown us no mercy. Anyway, when you're faced with overwhelming numbers you don't consider the morality of the issue. You just try to reduce the odds against you every chance you get. It's all down to the basic principle of kill or be killed.

'The Fascists didn't know what had hit them. They were pinned down on all sides. They couldn't even fire back. Their only hope was to find a well-protected hole somewhere in the broken terrain and wait for the Partisans to go away.

'The cries of the wounded were pitiful, but none of the Republican troops dared move to help a fallen comrade. Where possible, the Partisans would try to finish off a wounded man from the enemy force. Sometimes the Fascists turned their guns on their wounded friends to put them out of their misery.'

There was no gloating in Hope's description of the Partisans' overwhelming victory. Indeed I could detect a note of sadness as he recalled the scene of the hillside carnage. But as a soldier he could not disguise his admiration for the way Otello had marshalled his outnumbered troops.

As other members of his band continued to shoot at anything which moved higher up the hillside, sporadic shooting carried on all day long. But whereas the Partisans took their opportunities to snatch meal-breaks and the occasional forty winks, the demoralized Fascist troops remained frozen, literally and figuratively, in their foxholes.

The beleaguered soldiers of the Brigata Nera and the R.A.P. were further disillusioned when the messages they had sent seeking reinforcements were returned from Asti.

12 Rossana, now Mrs Pickering.

13 The author with Professor Max Salvadori and Guiseppe Fulcheri at the unveiling of a plaque in memory of John Keany at Cingalo, 24 April, 1988.

14 Settimo Maggiore at home, 1990.

They learned that the Germans had pulled out of the city and left it in the hands of Italian Fascists.

The writing was now clearly on the wall. The German withdrawal from Italy was gathering pace. It was changing from a carefully-planned and coordinated retreat to a full-scale flight for the border and the Devil take the hindmost.

Trapped in hostile territory, the Fascist troops on the hillside at Cisterna must have been terrified in spite of their superior, but dwindling, numbers. From Asti they heard that it was all their comrades could do to keep the local citizens in check, without breaking out to rescue a force of 1,500 well-equipped men from a bunch of 250-odd 'bandits'.

Night-time could not have come fast enough for these once-arrogant troops who had so recently called upon Otello and his band to surrender their lost cause. As the Partisans relaxed and took the opportunity for a well-earned rest, most of the Fascists managed to get away that night. By the morning they had retreated far enough to lick their wounds in Canale, leaving half their heavy artillery behind, regardless of the fact that it would fall into enemy hands. Nearly 200 dead still lay on the hillside.

Back in Canale, a group of 200 Fascists decided to call it a day and head back to their base in Turin. They could have taken any one of three roads, but they chose one which led through the village of San Stefano. As they set off in bright sunshine on the morning of 8 March, the men of the Brigata Nera must have been at a low ebb. Their convoy consisted of three drab-olive lorries, an armoured car and a military bus. A machine gun was mounted on the front of the armoured car, which contained six soldiers. All the other men were crammed into the three lorries and the bus.

The ubiquitous courier, Settimo Maggiorini, described to me what happened as the forlorn and battle-weary column limped unhappily back towards the refuge of Turin. They were observed by a Partisan called Carlo Tarditi, who owned a pony and trap. As soon as he saw which road the convoy had taken, Carlo raced ahead with his trotting pony down the rutted farm tracks. The Partisans had split into three groups to cover each road out of Canale. Just outside San

Stefano, one of these bands was told the Fascists were on their way by the breathless Carlo. Immediately other messengers were sent to bring the other two groups across to the road leading out of San Stefano.

'It was a perfect spot for an ambush,' said Settimo gleefully. 'The road was narrow as it wound its way out of the village with room for only one vehicle at a time. As the track led upwards we were all hiding on the left hand side of the convoy behind the acacia trees. Further along was a heavy machine gun at the top of a house which had a clear view over the hidden Partisans.

'When all the vehicles were out of the village and climbing uphill, the heavy machine gun opened up from a range of 400 metres. It could unload 200 rounds a minute and for a gun of that type it was the equivalent of point-blank range.

'The shells from our gun perforated the skin of the armoured car and flipped it over on to its right side as its driver lost control. The first burst from the heavy machine gun was the signal for the rest of our group to open fire. I was unarmed, but the others let rip with three light machine guns and their individual stens and rifles.

'As the Fascists jumped out of their lorries in their grey and black uniforms, they were cut down immediately. Grey helmets went cartwheeling down the rutted light brown soil, glittering in the weak spring sunshine, as their owners fell at the sides of the vehicles. Some of the Fascists managed to get to the far side of their lorries. But they didn't provide much shelter because the heavy machine-gun bullets could penetrate all but the thickest metal.

'Fire was returned but we were well dug-in and there was no accuracy in their shots. It was just a half-hearted effort aimed in our general direction. Our fire was more precise after the initial burst. We were picking out individual targets and it was becoming a slaughter. The roadside was turning into a reddish-brown colour from the blood which had been spilled. Although our hatred of the enemy was passionate and we knew they would have given us no quarter, I started to feel pity for them. Some were sprawling with hideous wounds. I can still hear their agonising screams whenever I think about what happened.

'After a few minutes of this carnage, some groups of Fascists held their hands up in the hope of surrender. Others were still firing. We looked to our commander, Lieutenant Chaka, for guidance. Chaka was the battle name of Francesco Cordero, a former sergeant in the Carabinieri. But before he could respond, three Partisans came out of cover to accept the surrender of an increasing number of soldiers who were throwing down their weapons and waving white handker-chiefs.

'What happened next was appalling. The three men — Bartolomeo Sola, Giacomo Curletto and Serafino Chiesa — stepped forward confidently. They had their guns at the ready and advanced towards a group who were offering themselves for surrender. But as they reached the foot of the bank which we were using as cover, there was a burst of fire from a group of Fascists crouched behind one of the trucks. This devastating and unexpected hail of bullets from close range killed our three comrades instantly. Whether the Fascists knew they had moved forward to accept a surrender or whether they believed they were moving in for the kill, we shall never know. But the sight of our colleagues being shot down like that stiffened our resolve and our hatred of the soldiers. Without waiting for Chaka's approval, our men poured fire into the truck from where the fighting Fascists had sent their deadly volley.

'The guilty men paid a quick price for their deeds as they were hit by a fusillade of machine-gun and rifle bullets. Within seconds half-a-dozen more soldiers had paid the ulti-mate price and added to the reddish-brown pool which was seeping like an oil slick over the area.

'It was too late now for our fallen comrades, but there was an intense feeling of satisfaction among the rest of us that their deaths had been so swiftly avenged.

'By now the leader of the Fascist convoy was waving a white flag from his car which had reached the rear of the patrol. He could see his position was hopeless. There was no way for his men to escape. Furthermore, apart from the

117

tragic deaths of the three Partisans whose over-enthusiasm had led them from cover, the Republican soldiers were dying in vain in a one-sided contest. Chaka had selected such a perfect spot for the ambush that he could pick off his opponents without risk to his own men.

'Soon all firing ceased from the convoy and white hankies and bandages fluttered in upraised hands everywhere. The eyes of the Partisans swung towards Chaka for instructions. He held up his hand to signal us to cease firing. Within seconds every man had obeyed his command. The comparative silence made the cries of the dying and the badly wounded more heart-rending. Then Chaka shouted to the Fascist leader, "Tell your men to throw down all their weapons and move forward away from the vehicles."

'The leader of the Fascists sought an assurance that his men would not be harmed. "You are in no position to seek any bargains," said Chaka, "and if there is any treachery I give my solemn promise you will all die."

'The Fascist leader realized he could not argue. He ordered his men to lay down their arms and move out into the open with their hands aloft. Then Chaka signalled his men to move slowly forward, guns at the ready, to make sure there was no further "misunderstanding." They went round the vehicles and checked. An arsenal of weapons was collected and brought back to the ridge where the rest of the Partisans were covering the prisoners. Then Chaka came down to talk to his opposite number. It seemed he and the Fascist leader had served together before and at the start of the war. Chaka gave him a lecture about how he had chosen the wrong side and how all good Italians should abandon Mussolini and his German pals in favour of the Partisans.

'While they were talking, our men gave the prisoners a good roughing up. It was no more than they deserved. As far as we were concerned they all shared in the blame for the deaths of Bartolomeo, Giacomo and Serafino. We had also heard that they had killed another brave Partisan earlier that day. He was a teenager called Domencio Bergamasco whom they had captured. Despite intensive questioning,

Domencio had told his captors he would rather die than give them information about his comrades. So the Brigata Nera shot him.

'There were many Partisans in our force who would have been in favour of shooting the prisoners, because we couldn't afford to keep them. We had no facilities for dealing with such a large number − more than 100 men had survived the ambush.

'Chaka decided that after the previously uninjured Fascists had been given a good beating and after they had been stripped of their weapons, we should leave them to get back to Turin as best they could. We collected their guns and the bodies of our three dead comrades and headed back to Cisterna. We felt we had taught the Fascists a decisive lesson.'

As Settimo told me the story of the Partisans' success, I was furious that I had missed out on all the glory. I was full of admiration for the way they had out-thought and out-fought the enemy. But I was green with envy to think that I had missed all that action.

My feeling was that my own fighting after Keany's death had been merely a combination of evasion and running away. I realized that discretion was the better part of valour, but the behaviour of the Partisans was more in line with my idea of warfare than the inauspicious skirmishing which I had experienced. Throughout the day I kept comparing the circumstances. And that night, as we joined in the songs around the campfire, I came to my conclusion.

The Italians certainly know how to celebrate a victory. Campfires were lit all around the castle at Cisterna. Weary fighting men now found a second wind as the adrenalin caused by danger successfully overcome pumped through their bloodstreams and mingled with the copious quantities of red wine. I joined in as best I could with all the songs they sang. The Partisans had a natural harmony, like a Welsh male-voice choir, and the scenery was every bit as breathtaking as any you could find in the mountains and valleys of Wales.

With the stars twinkling overhead, it was a bitterly cold night. But the Partisans draped thick blankets over their shoulders and huddled close to the cooking fires for warmth.

There was little to eat except for a gooey cauldron of polenta, but even that tasted better in victory.

The food may have been in short supply, but there was a steady flow of red wine which was passed around from group to group in a most companionable way. I was with Millard, Hope, Roccia and other Partisan leaders. We were being feted by the Bandits of Cisterna for the part we had played in arming and supplying them. Time and time again these swarthy fellows would embrace us and thank us profusely for our help. As the night wore on and the wine continued to pass around our group, the embraces became more affectionate, the vows of eternal friendship more effusive and the smell of alcohol more overpowering. I did not mind at all. I had become drunk with the atmosphere of that evening long before the wine took its toll. And as the songs became more ragged and bawdy, the more I soaked up this carnival spirit.

Hope and Roccia entered fully into the joy of the occasion, although I suspect they were discreet enough to take smaller swigs than Millard and myself when the flasks came round later.

The celebrations went on till dawn, with many of the revellers falling asleep at the side of their fires and staying warm by the embers.

Our two senior officers turned in just before sunrise, leaving Millard and I to continue the carousing. They must have sensed that, after my experience with Keany the day before, it made psychological sense for me to get plastered. It was also good for me to have my old drinking buddy 'Busty' Millard for company.

The Partisans seemed to understand my situation as well. They are a more passionate and emotional people than the British. Consequently, at times like these, they were just what the doctor ordered for me.

'So what you do now?' one of them asked.

'That's a good question,' I replied. 'There's no point in going to Milan now Captain Keany's dead. And there's no way of going back to the Allied lines. I seem to be stuck here.'

My Partisan friend then held a whispered conversation with his comrades. I could sense they were talking about me because from time to time they would look in my direction and weigh me up and down. Then they nodded in agreement. Hands were raised as if a vote had been taken. The decision was unanimous. Their spokesman shuffled back over to me on his haunches and asked, 'Would you like to join us?'

I did not understand the question. I was already on their side, helping them to fight Mussolini and the Fascists.

'What do you mean, join you?' I inquired.

He grinned. 'Join the Partisans,' he said. 'Become one of the Bandits of Cisterna.'

It took a little while to sink in. These simple-spirited, stout-hearted men had recognized my loss in the death of Keany. They wanted to rescue me from my despair and give me a new sense of purpose.

'Will I join the Bandits of Cisterna?' I asked. 'Oh yes. Too bloody true.'

I beamed with delight. Then I fell asleep by the side of the campfire.

VIII

DEATH AND DESTRUCTION

The dawn sunshine had dribbled over the hillside, poured into the valley and the spring sun was standing high in a cloudless sky when I awoke from the night's revelries. Around me groups of Partisans were shaking themselves like spaniels and wiping the remainder of the dew off their dishevelled clothing.

I surveyed the scene through bleary eyes and remembered my final conversation. In my befuddled state, I began to plan a strategic campaign to persuade Major Hope to allow me to become a brigand. It was not going to be easy.

As I made my way to the washing and shaving facilities in the castle, I pondered the best course of action. Busty Millard had been having great difficulties in sending out and receiving transmissions. It would be easy to put myself forward as an alternative or supportive radio operator; but that could result in my being trapped at base, missing out on all the action again.

Slowly a brainwave began to seep into my throbbing head and suggest itself as the answer to my problems. I could assert that my radio transmitter appeared to be better than that of Millard. Consequently, if I could use my experience with my set to show Millard how to obtain the best results, the pair of us could share the workload.

My scheme was to persuade Hope to let us take it in turns to use the transmitter, knowing we could work it between ourselves to our mutual advantage and convenience. Feeling well pleased with myself, considerably improved in appearance and fast recovering from the excesses of the previous night, I presented myself to Major Hope in the castle at Cisterna.

He took me quickly into a private room and invited me to sit down. This was usually the prelude to some unexpected bad news, so I braced myself for the worst.

'Glad you came, Pickering,' said Hope in his clipped tones. 'I'm afraid I've got another spot of unpleasant tidings for you.'

My mind started racing as Hope continued in his irritatingly long-winded fashion.

'You were friendly with the Partisan Rino Rossino, weren't you?'

I nodded. Rossino and I had played cards together as partners and shared the odd flask of wine during my earlier stay at Cisterna with Keany. Hope's use of the past tense in referring to Rino had already prepared me for what I was about to hear.

'Well I'm afraid we heard that, while you were away, the Brigata Nera caught him, took him into a village square and shot him as an example to the locals. It was a terrible thing to happen, but Rossino died as he had lived. He gave nothing away and spat defiance at them to the end. I had heard that you and Rossino were friends and I'm sure that you and Captain Keany must have become very close too. You've probably gone through the wringer emotionally in the last 48 hours, but I think the best thing for you now, Pickering, is to keep busy. I want you to work as a radio operator here in Cisterna. How would you feel about that?'

I could hardly believe my ears. For once in my life, I was actually being asked to do something I wanted to do. It was all I could manage to stop myself from beaming with delight and shaking the Major's hand. Instead I tried to look pensive.

Looking at him gravely, I replied, 'Thank you, sir. Of course I will do anything I'm ordered to do, sir. But I do have a favour to ask. Will it be possible to show Millard how my transmitter works and share my duties with him? You see, I got about quite a bit with Captain Keany and I know my way around the place quite well now. I think I could be useful to the Partisans, sir, and I feel I need to do something active to avenge the deaths of my comrades.' I knew this last remark would appeal to Hope's strong feeling of esprit de corps.

Hope smiled. 'That's what I like to see in a soldier, Pickering,' he said, 'but on this occasion it's not exactly what I want to hear. Let me put it to you this way, Pickering. If we can get our messages in and out of Cisterna, then I'll be happy. There'll be times when I'll need you — and nobody else but you — to go out with me on missions. At other times, if you want to use your free time to go off on your own, that's up to you. I don't want to know about it. And let me make one thing abundantly clear. If anything goes wrong, you're on your own. You don't have any official permission to go off with your Partisan chums. This conversation has not taken place. But I know how you must feel and I wish you the very best of luck.'

He shook me by the hand and started to lead me out of the sparsely-furnished room.

'Just one more thing, Pickering,' he muttered as we walked away together. 'Don't, under any circumstances, get yourself shot.'

I grinned. 'Of course not, sir,' I replied.

'And that's an order,' he barked as he wheeled away from me.

I could hardly contain my delight. I virtually ran to the farmhouse shippon where Millard had been billeted. When I arrived he was still struggling to get through on his set, sending and receiving signals too weak to be heard.

Without further ado I unslung my machine, lobbed the wire out of the window on to a nearby tree, and said, 'Now watch very carefully, Busty. You're going to be doing a lot of this in the next few days.'

As I went through the routine with Busty, I told him of my recent conversation with Hope and the earlier one with my new unofficial regiment, the Bandits of Cisterna.

Millard soon learned the idiosyncrasies of my set. In a couple of hours of tuition he was as capable of working it as well as I could. By leaving it tuned to the precise frequencies required, I had complete confidence that he could stand in for me at any time and leave me free to pursue my own adventures.

When I told the Partisans I had been given unofficial permission to join them, they were as thrilled as I was. I became known as 'Inglese Billy' and I was an honoured guest at their pow-wows when they discussed their various missions.

I discovered that their most pressing task of the moment was the rebuilding of a landing strip at Vesime. This was to be one of the most audacious schemes in the history of the Second World War. The plan was simple. An airfield which had been ploughed up by the Germans to make it unusable was to be secretly restored. A group of shot-down American airmen were to be smuggled to the landing strip at the precise moment when an Allied plane was to make a daring daylight landing. Then, as the Partisans kept the enemy at bay, it would take off again and fly everybody back behind the Allied lines.

I had already met the leader of one of the groups of American fliers, Group Bombardier Jack Temple, on my earlier visit to Cisterna. He had told me how anti-aircraft guns had brought down his B25 bomber when it tried to destroy a bridge at Casale Monferrato. Temple, a handsome young volunteer from Kansas, was in the lead plane of a 'plover' formation of fifty-four aircraft from the 379th bomber group. It was his thirtieth mission after fifteen as navigator, ten as squadron bombardier and the previous four as group bombardier. As group leader he accompanied the pilot in the first plane as they led the bombing team over its target. It was the anniversary of Armistice Day, 11 November, 1944. They had been told the bridge was a vital escape route for a convoy of S.S. troops heading north.

Temple had described to me earlier how his plane had been shot down and the battle which followed as the Partisans tried to rescue the airmen from under the noses of the German ground forces.

'I was operating the Norden bombsight when our plane was hit by anti-aircraft fire,' explained Temple. 'It knocked away our right engine and blew the glass out of the B25's nose. Our waist gunner, Joe Glydon, was injured by shrapnel, so we applied first-aid dressing to his wounds and tossed him out of the escape hatch as carefully as time would allow. We later learned that Joe had been captured by the Nazis when his parachute landed because his injuries made it impossible for him to get away. The rest of us were spread all over Piedmont.'

Another of the crew in Temple's plane later gave his description of what happened on that fateful day. Navigator Constantine 'George' Mitchell was a store clerk in New London, Connecticut, when the army drafted him in 1941.

'I was assigned to a quartermaster's outfit, a real cushy billet,' said Mitchell. But in 1942 he applied to become an air force cadet and by 1944 Lieutenant Mitchell was stationed in Corsica, bombing targets throughout Italy. His navigational skills ultimately won him a Silver Star, a Distinguished Flying Cross and a Purple Heart, but on 11 November, 1944, he was flying his 78th mission, two trips short of earning an automatic return ticket to America.

Mitchell's orders were to steer the B25 to a railroad bridge across the River Po at Casale Monferrato. American bombers had already destroyed sixteen of the river's twenty bridges, so the Nazis had concentrated all their ack-ack guns around the remainder.

It was getting more dangerous with every bridge we knocked out,' said Mitchell. 'Our squadron set off on the 11th hour of the 11th day of the 11th month − the exact moment of the armistice signing in 1918. We were hit on the way in and the way out. The shrapnel was bouncing all over the place like marbles.

'We held our course and scored several direct hits, rendering the bridge useless. But one of our two engines caught fire and Gunner Joe Glydon was struck in the leg. I was too busy bandaging his wound to notice I had been nicked on the wrist as well. Meanwhile our pilot, Laverne Hacking, had put out the fire and was trying to reach the sea on one engine. But the plane dipped below the level of the mountains so we had to bale out. We helped to throw Joe out and then followed in his wake. I landed in a tree. My parachute caught and I was dangling some five or six feet off the ground. I was completely helpless as a Fiat approached me. It contained several men inside with more standing on the fender. They were carrying carbines and grenades.

'I remember thinking "I've had it now." But they shouted "Friends. Amici. Friends. Amici."

'They pulled me down and asked politely if they could have my white silk parachute. I said, "Sure", and asked them why they wanted it. One of them explained, "It makes beautiful wedding gowns". I was so relieved to still be alive that I thought this was the funniest thing I had ever heard. I laughed hysterically and they must have thought they had rescued a lunatic.'

Mitchell described how the Partisans drove him to a hilltop farmhouse where he was reunited with six of his fellow crew members. Glydon needed proper medical attention and had been left on a road where he was picked up by the Nazis.

The airmen ate and drank with their rescuers until they heard the sound of shooting nearby. Then the crew were divided into twos and threes. A guide ran down the hill with Mitchell and Hacking. They just crested another in time to elude the pursuing Germans who had reached the farmhouse.

Partisans from Otello's division told me how they kept the German soldiers at bay long enough to evacuate the airmen from the area in small manageable groups. It was Otello's Asti Brigade who reached them minutes before a strong force of Jerries were despatched to capture them. They started firing too soon and lost the element of surprise over the Partisans without achieving any hits. Skirmishing went on all day till evening when the Germans withdrew, removing their dead and wounded. They also took Glydon to hospital in Asti.

Four men were wounded from the brigade's San Damiano group, which was led by an adjutant called Francesco Bellero, who fought under the battle name of 'Gris'. He was supported by his formidable wife Olga, who was known as 'Grisa'. She looked like a mixture of Boadicea and Pancho Villa as she toted her sub-machine gun and stood fearlessly in the front line with ammunition belts criss-crossed diagonally over her shoulders. Even when her youngest son Chiaffredo was shot in the leg, Grisa carried on fighting. She supervised his removal to a place of safety for attention and then rushed back to the fray with her gun blazing. Grisa was a source of inspiration to her comrades as she bustled along the line, distributing ammo and encouragement. Happily her son, who had joined his two elder brothers in the Partisans shortly after his 16th birthday and was 18 when he was wounded, made a full recovery.

The American airmen were smuggled away out of the area and spent the next three months evading capture. Mitchell described their existence as they lived with the Partisans behind enemy lines.

'We slept in caves, barns and, occasionally, a house,' he said. 'We were comfortable most of the time. The more animals a barn had, the warmer it was. We got to rating the accommodation for its warmth and comfort. The poor quality ones only got a one-cow rating, but a five-cow barn was our equivalent of the Hilton Hotel.

'One time a guide was leading Hacking and I down a road when a German guard called out "Who goes there?" in German. We froze but the Partisan began to chatter away in German, while casually approaching the soldier. Then "Boom." He shot the German right in the guts. The three of us jumped over an embankment and fled into the woods.

'We met one of your British intelligence officers who directed drops of food, clothing and weapons. It was arranged for us to be rescued by torpedo boat in the spring. But the Nazis sealed off the valley we were in one day in February and combed it from one end to the other. A family offered to hide me and Hacking in their barn, but we didn't want to get them shot on our account. We decided to try to make it through the woods to the sea, but a German search party caught us. We were taken north through a series of county and state jails.

'It was a treacherous journey. Allied aircraft strafed captors and prisoners alike on the road, and even bombed one of our jails. I remember we had to go down to this shelter six storeys deep with all these Germans. Our bombers made spurts of dirt come out of the side of the shelter even at that depth. I tell you I was more scared then than I was when we were shot down.'

Mitchell said he was treated decently by the German Army, although they came in for some rough handling in camps run by the S.S.

'One of these Gestapo officers was interrogating me and he knocked me to the ground,' Mitchell recalled. 'When I got up with my fists instinctively raised, he set his dog on me.'

Mitchell ended the war with 66,000 other prisoners at Stalag 7A in Moosburg, Germany.

'By the end of the war the local bakery had been bombed and the only food left was soup with something mysterious floating in it,' said Mitchell.

'We were liberated in April, 1945, and General George Patton came to the stalag a day later. I remember he had a big smile. He was a handsome fellow with a pair of pearl-handled revolvers. Patton told us, "I'll get you out of here this week. I don't know how but I will." He promptly found some cargo planes in Britain and had them airlift 50 to 100 soldiers per flight. Otherwise we might have been sitting around for three or four months.'

Mitchell returned to America and was discharged as a captain. He thought he had led an exciting life with Hacking evading the Germans — until he heard what had happened to the rest of his crew!

They had managed to evade capture throughout that harsh winter, and now I was brought into the extraordinary plan to get them back behind the Allied lines. Not just Group Bombardier Temple and his three colleagues, mind you. We were also arranging for eight other airmen who had made a forced landing at Turin Airport to be flown back 'home' as well. And just for good measure, at the last moment, we arranged for two escaped prisoners to hitch a lift back too.

The other airmen were from a heavy bomber squadron on their second or third mission who had become lost or disorientated in their B24 over the Alps somewhere near the

Brenner Pass. The pilot was low on fuel and sought the nearest available spot to land. He picked the enemy-occupied Turin Airport for his emergency landing, but once again the Partisans were quicker to react to the unexpected than their German counterparts. The Partisans spirited the American airmen away and delivered them to the small hotel in San Damiano where anti-Fascist guards and S.O.E. money was keeping Jack Temple.

The brief for the Bandits of Cisterna was to rebuild a landing site in a ploughed field at Vesime. We had simultaneously arranged for a C-47 to land on the strip while the air crews were brought to the meadow. Then while the Partisans stood guard, the plane would fly its precious cargo back to an Allied-held airfield at Siena.

It all sounded quite feasible in theory. I decided it would be interesting to see how things worked out in practice. As we sat around the campfire that night, we decided it was vital to keep the nearby Fascist garrisons occupied with a series of guerrilla raids, starting the following night.

I sent the day's messages back to base and left Millard in charge while I went off duty. Then I met my comrades as arranged near the church at Cisterna. We set off at dusk on a moonless night.

There were six men in our group, including me. We were all armed to the teeth. In addition I had my battledress pockets stuffed with plastic explosive. I had handed the detonators to our group leader Nino just to be on the safe side.

Nino was about the same age as me, but he was definitely in charge of our little band. Two of his men were approaching middle age, but they were content to accept Nino's authority. I was just happy to be going along for the ride. In fact the ride turned out to be a three-hour walk along deserted country roads and across fields. One of the older Partisans seemed to be leading the way and we followed at a discreet distance. Nino had already told us our objective — a main rail link near one of the local stations.

Apart from the usual barking of farmyard dogs, we encountered no signs of life during our journey. Then we saw the dim lights of the blacked-out station ahead of us.

Nino had told me how the station-master was a sympathizer who was happy to provide the Partisans with intelligence about the movement of troops and goods. On this occasion he had sent a message to Nino informing him that a train carrying a dangerous load was due to pass through his station at 11 p.m.

We had no idea what the Fascists would have on board, but we gambled that it would be explosives. Our aim was to put on a firework display for the local farmers. The station-master's message had included a special request that we should keep our action at least half a mile away from his precious premises. As he slept there, I suppose he had a point.

It was 9.30 p.m. when we reached the station. Nino indicated we should all stop talking and proceed with our plan in silence. One of our group remained out of sight at the station to keep lookout while we crept silently along the track. Another of the Partisans walked fifty yards ahead of us as we moved from sleeper to sleeper for half a mile. Then our scout took up his position 200 yards beyond the point where we intended to blow up the train. Two of the others climbed the embankment on either side while Nino and I went to work. I spread the plastic explosive along both lines. Then I showed Nino where to place the detonators so they would be set off on impact as the train went over them. The entire process took less than five minutes

Our job complete, I signalled to the two nearest lookouts, while Nino brought back the other Partisan from further along the track with an owl-like hoot. While he covered our rear from a distance, Nino went ahead of the three of us. As we neared the station Nino gave another low hoot. It was returned by the comrade we had left on guard and we saw him emerge from a hedgerow. We grinned and gave him the thumbs-up sign. Then we circled round the fields to take up a vantage point.

I felt like a kid on Bonfire Night. It had started to drizzle to strengthen the impression that we had lit the blue touch-paper and retired. I was bursting with excitement to see the results of our handiwork.

As the minutes ticked away towards 11 o'clock, the tension mounted. We were checking our watches every few moments as the hour grew nearer. Then came the anti-climax. Eleven o'clock came and went, as did five past, ten past and quarter past without any signs of a train. My memory now turned to the Bonfire Night damp squibs and the disappointment engendered when a firework failed to explode.

Then we heard a faint rumbling noise in the distance. A train was approaching the station. It stopped for what seemed like an eternity while parcels were taken on board. Then, after a five-minute delay, it set off in the direction of our 'bombe surprise'. There were only six coaches on the train. It was a goods vehicle but we were in no position to see the contents as it trundled past some 300 yards away, slowly gathering speed.

I feel sure we were all doing individual mental calculations of when it would reach the point of no return. I recall feeling dismayed for some five seconds when I believed the train had passed our explosive devices without detonating them. But then we heard a muffled bang as the weight of the train triggered off the detonators. For a split second we held our communal breath, then there was a blinding flash of light, swiftly followed by the most almighty roar.

The locomotive seemed at first to have passed the point of danger unscathed, but then the first goods wagon leapt into the air, pulling the locomotive up with it. For a few seconds we were able to watch the slow-motion destruction of the train as each wagon tried to climb over the back of its leader. Then a second, third and fourth explosion came in quick succession as the contents of the wagons were ignited by the fire cause by the initial blast. The heavy vehicles were hurled many feet into the air and we looked on in wonder as they spun around like toys.

I was spellbound until Nino gave me a dig in the ribs. Grinning from ear to ear, he said, 'Not bad, Inglese. You know what you're doing.' Then he ushered us away from the gloriously devastating scene.

As we hurried off into the night, with the sound of further

explosions diminishing in the background, I had not the nerve to tell Nino this was the first time I had used explosives in anger; that until this night I had only practised with fish!

Our scout led the way again as we headed back to Cisterna. Our spirits were soaring when we returned at 3 a.m. It had been a long day, but I was too excited to sleep. Our group shared a flask of wine round a fire just outside the castle.

'So,' I inquired. 'What's on the agenda for tomorrow?'

But it was another couple of days before my next Partisans' outing. Their control of the rural areas was being consolidated all the time after the crucial battle of Cisterna. We felt confident enough to move about cautiously in broad daylight.

So it was that Nino and his gang led me by truck and then on foot to the field at Vesime. It was a sloping meadow some 500 yards long and 100 yards across. At the end of the slight incline stood a tree, roughly 12 inches thick and 25 feet high. The field was generally flat, but it had been ploughed up deliberately by the occupying German troops whose use for it as an emergency landing base was long since over. Although new grass was starting to sprout through the soil, it was clear that any plane which tried to land there would flip over and bury itself in the softer earth.

The Partisans had three problems to overcome. Firstly they had to level the field again and make sure it was universally firm. Secondly they had to do the work without being spotted by the Fascist soldiers or their informers. And thirdly they had to carry out the work without leaving any trace or telltale signs of what they were doing.

Nino estimated it would take a week to prepare the field, and that by working under the cover of darkness we were unlikely to arouse any suspicions. But the risks of the half-finished job being noticed by a Fascist patrol seemed high.

After visiting the site, I discussed the problem with Major Hope. He, in turn, talked about the situation with Roccia and Hugh Ballard, the no-nonsense South African who had met us on our landing at Mombarcaro and who had been promoted to major because of his sterling work with the Partisans in the Cuneo area.

The tough-talking Ballard listened intently as I described the airstrip and the nature of the difficulties we would have to face. I told them how Nino reckoned we could complete the task in a week.

'How many men will he be using?' asked Ballard.

'I think he was counting on about a dozen, sir,' I replied.

'What if he had a hundred men?' Ballard inquired. 'How long would that take?'

Ballard's question was so simple and so obviously straight to the point that it took me by surprise. This could be the answer to all our problems. We brought Otello into the discussions and asked if he could spare a massive work detail.

Eventually a plan was devised. Small, imperceptible improvements would be made to the ploughed field ready for a frantic 48-hour effort before the landing. Labour-intensive toil would start at dusk two nights before the landing was due. It would continue under strict security throughout the next day and night and would be completed within 48 hours, just before the rescue plane arrived. Security would involve the total encirclement of the area with armed Partisans and an elaborate system of discreet messages to warn of approaching Fascist forces.

At one stage Hope suggested a series of smoke signals could be used, Apache style, to raise the alarm. For one awful moment I was reminded of the madcap schemes of Major Munthe. Happily, on this occasion, sanity prevailed and we decided to use more conventional methods. Mobile units of Partisans, armed to the teeth with machine guns, grenades and even anti-tank weapons, would be scattered around the area when the time came. If a patrol stumbled within a three-mile radius of the landing strip, they would be attacked with everything we had.

Other Partisans would be despatched to bring the individual airmen to the field at the appointed hour. My job would be to take charge of communications in the liaison between the S.O.E. organizers and the Partisans, and between our field operators and base H.Q.

Meanwhile it was imperative that the Bandits of Cisterna should retain the initiative they had earned in battle and keep up the pressure on the demoralized forces of Fascism. Otello readily agreed that we should use the intervening period to increase our attacks on their supply routes and patrols.

'They are already like children — afraid of the dark,' he gloated. 'Now we must make them afraid of the daytime as well. I promise you that by the time your plane lands, the cowardly Fascist bullies will be too frightened to set foot outside their cities. The people are sick of them. More and more are flocking to join us every day.' And so the strategy was devised. But as soon as I was freed from my S.O.E. duties, I delegated to Millard and became 'Inglese Billy' again.

Now it was time to discuss guerrilla tactics with Nino. He was like a naughty schoolboy when it came to discussing ambushes or sabotage. To hear him chuckle gleefully you would think he was scrumping for apples in an orchard or playing knock and run rather than facing a deadly foe. His boyish enthusiasm was infectious, even if the elder members of his gang did shake their heads from time to time at his gung-ho exuberance.

Nino, and group leaders like him, had been instructed by Otello to bring him ideas for pressurizing the Fascists. In this way Otello ensured that the right hand always knew what the left was doing and that none of his beloved bandits would inadvertently attack each other through lack of communication. It also caused a form of creative rivalry among the leaders to invent and plan a string of attacks. They considered it a great honour if Otello accepted their suggestions, thereby increasing their prestige.

It took Nino a week to come up with an acceptable plan and he was flushed with excitement when he received Otello's seal of approval. Nino was being fed information from a Partisan sympathizer who cooked meals for the Fascists at Asti. There was always a danger of falling victim to a double agent, but this chef's reliability had already been put to the test. So when Nino heard from him that a patrol of Republican soldiers was planning a thorough *rastrellamento* in a village five miles away, he leapt into action. Instead of moving all the Partisan supporters out of the village to avoid the danger, Nino suggested moving men in! His idea was sound. The Fascists invariably sent men quietly to the back of a suspect village before marching the main force in the front. Anybody trying to run away at the first sight of the app-roaching soldiers would plunge headlong into the carefully-laid trap. Nino's plan was to set a snare for the trappers and see how the Fascists fared when they found themselves outnumbered for once in their lives.

Nino told us how his spy had discovered that the patrol would be moving out of Asti at first light. They would be twenty-strong and five of them were being detached to slip to the back of the village. There they would take up positions where they could shoot anybody trying to flee. The main force of fifteen would then march forward and terrorize the cowering inhabitants. On this occasion, however, the Republican soldiers would not find a bunch of terrified civ-ilians. They would be faced by a formidable force of battle-hardened Partisans who had been armed to the teeth by a series of S.O.E. air drops.

We drove into the village crammed inside two ancient trucks which had been 'liberated' from the Germans. There were about forty of us in all. After we had sealed off the area, Nino approached a house where a known and trusted Parti-san supporter lived with his family, where he established that there were no villagers with Fascist sympathies and could rest assured that nobody would give the game away. Safe in that knowledge, we hid our vehicles carefully off the road (which was little more than a farm track) and took up positions in the buildings.

A couple of other Partisan leaders outranked young Nino on the mission, but they were happy to give their protégé his head and allow him to take unofficial charge of the pro-ceedings. His grimy face shone with pride.

The inhabitants reacted in a positive manner to the noctur-nal disturbances. Any lingering doubts that the population supported the Partisans and hated the Fascists were dispelled by what happened that night. Poor people who were barely scratching an existence for themselves brought food and wine out for us. It was humble fare, but it might just as well have been champagne and caviar as far as I was concerned.

The Partisans moved their equipment into position in bedrooms and living rooms of the stone-built, whitewashed houses and cottages. Villagers helped them to carry the ammunition into place, even though the disposition of the weapons made it likely that any return of fire would result in bullets ripping through their windows and furniture. Women, children and the more ancient inhabitants were evacuated from the village to I know not where. The able-bodied men refused to leave and demanded weapons. They wanted their hour of glory too.

Those staying in the village were advised to grab forty winks while they awaited the arrival of the opposing team. I was despatched with Nino's gang and some fresh faces to take up position on the road leading out of the village. Nino had plotted where the Fascists would be bound to set their trap and he wanted us in place a few yards behind their positions.

It worked like a dream. We bedded down till dawn, then instinctively awoke to carry out our ablutions and await the arrival of the enemy. Unlike the train ten days earlier, the blue-uniformed troops arrived right on schedule.

One of the most difficult objectives for any group of people is to stay absolutely quiet for hours on end. The ability to do so of the Partisans and those of us trained by the S.O.E. was to prove crucial time and time again. On this occasion we heard the discreet approach of the five Republican 'back-markers' when they were about 100 yards away. In the silence their whispering sounded like shouts and their heavy tread through the undergrowth seemed to be magnified by loudspeakers.

Exactly as Nino had planned, they took up their predicted positions. If they had been actors moving towards their chalked stage places, they could not have performed better for us. Then one of them announced into his radio: 'Rear party in position. Ready when you are'.

137

That was the signal Nino had been waiting for. As soon as he heard it, Nino motioned his men forward. As the Fascists lit cigarettes and chatted to each other, they were impervious to the deadly danger which was creeping up on them. The vital target was the man with the radio, but it was also fundamental to the success of Nino's plan that no shots should be fired. None were necessary. When the Fascist radio operator had his throat cut from behind and two of his colleagues were garrotted, their two lucky comrades offered no resistance to the daggers held at their necks.

From the safety of the trees I was happy to report the complete triumph of the first part of the plan. I sent a signal to a Partisan inside the village that the Fascist trappers at the rear were *hors de combat*.

I believe the two senior Partisan leaders had used their expertise and experience to set a classic pincer movement upon the unsuspecting advancing Fascists. The troops had disembarked from their lorries about a mile from the village. Then fifteen of them waited for half an hour while their colleagues crept into position at the rear.

After receiving the message that their comrades were 'in position', they walked confidently up the track leading to the village. This was probably a sound tactic, if your purpose was to act like grouse-beaters, driving your quarry towards the shooters' butts at the back of the village. Little did they know they were marching arrogantly towards a fearsome foe who were straining at the proverbial leash.

I heard later that night, at what had become the traditional celebratory party, what happened in the village after we had taken care of the rearguard.

A well-educated English-speaking Partisan described the scene as the Fascist soldiers marched towards the village:

'They made the classic mistake of taking things for granted,' he said with a grin. 'They swaggered towards us with no semblance of discipline. They had no advance scouts. Perhaps they wanted to be spotted so any guilty Partisans would run towards what they thought was their trap. As they sauntered into firing range we held back until they were well and truly inside the jaws of the wolf. Then we let them have it with everything. They never stood a chance.

'Three-quarters of them were wiped out with our first volley, and the rest only managed to scamper into ditches which we had covered anyway. I can't remember a single shot being fired back in our direction. We could have wiped out all of them if we had so desired. But we were happy to allow two or three of them back to Asti like frightened rabbits.

'Of course we had requisitioned their two lorries so they had to run back as fast as their legs could carry them. We had decided earlier that it was helpful to our overall strategy if some survived to return to base to spread alarm and despondency among their comrades.'

Both members of the Fascist rearguard we had captured expressed a keen desire to join the Partisans. How much of this was born out of a will to survive and how much was through genuine conversion to the anti-Fascist cause one can only speculate.

Otello greeted us like heroes on our return. We had given the Fascists another reason to stay indoors and keep them from poking their noses into what was happening at Vesime. He hugged each of us personally and thanked us for our efforts. Otello had that rare quality of leadership – the ability to make every single one of us feel special.

I was exhausted but exhilarated by the time Otello had welcomed us back to Cisterna. As the wine flasks passed around and the patriotic songs were sung, it felt good to be 'a bandit'.

A few days later I negotiated some time off with Busty and headed for the hills again with my new comrades. This time we set off at dusk on foot for San Damiano, where the target was the railway station.

Dino Tartaglino, a thick-set local butcher with black, wavy hair, was in charge of the expedition. When our small band from Cisterna met him at midnight at a farm building a mile from the station he outlined his plans. There were twenty-five of us and he estimated a similar number of Fascist soldiers were guarding the station. The Partisans had managed to place a suitcase full of plastic explosives, primed with a timing device, next to the barracks of the sleeping soldiers in a converted waiting room. The rest of us were to take up positions forming a crescent round one side of the station, armed with bazookas and machine guns.

When the bomb went off, that was our signal to open up with our light artillery. We had been waiting an hour when a blinding flash illuminated the starless sky, the ground shook and a crack like thunder threatened to burst our eardrums 250 yards away. I can only guess at the effect this had on the luckless occupants. Fortunately the station-master was a Partisan sympathizer who had made his own arrangements to avoid the initial explosion and the devastating attack which followed.

The firing lasted for less than a minute and the enemy reply must have amounted to less than a dozen rounds. Stunned by our surprise salvo, they did not wait for any cessation in the hostilities. Without so much as a white flag to shield them, the Republican soldiers rushed out with their hands aloft, shouting, 'Don't shoot. We surrender.' The night guards were in full dark blue uniform but some of their comrades were just wearing trousers and boots with their braces dangling loosely round their knees.

Four Fascists died in our raid and another two officers and thirteen men were taken prisoner. One of them was shaking from head to foot like a jelly. He appeared to have caught the blast of an explosion in his face. There was not much blood apart from tiny lacerations. But his head had swollen up like a giant white balloon to create a grotesque, wobbling figure.

We guessed that some of the enemy soldiers must have escaped across the far side of the railway line taking their wounded with them. It was now the job of Nino and his men, including me, to march our prisoners back to the castle at Cisterna.

The Partisans had taken no casualties at all in the attack but this did not prevent them from giving their prisoners a hard time. With brutal shoves and rifle butts they urged the sullen Fascists along as we trekked homewards.

Dawn had broken when we reached Cisterna with our 'bag'. Some of those captured would volunteer to join the fight against Fascism while others would be used in exchange for Partisan prisoners in due course. Otello was delighted with our night's work.

It was eight days before I went into action with the Partisans again. In the meantime I heard a progress report on the situation at Vesime, which was becoming of increasing importance as more Allied airmen and escaped prisoners arrived in the area to await evacuation.

During this intervening period I learned that the airstrip had been used the previous summer and autumn by Lysander light reconnaissance planes. These were high-wing monoplanes suitable for landing and picking up single agents because of the short take-off and touch-down space required. They were also capable of operating on rougher ground than that needed by the heavier Dakotas.

An S.O.E. hero named Neville Darewski, relative of famous bandleader Herman Darewski, had first spotted the potential of the airstrip at Vesime. Under his battle name of Major Temple, he had organized a series of ammunition drops as head of the Special Force mission to the Mauri group. Major Temple had also supervised the discreet comings and goings of many of our agents in the Lysander. I had met him in the summer of 1944 when he was recruiting a radio operator for his mission. He had interviewed me at Monopoli, but my youth counted against me and he chose a man named Farrimond instead.

The winter snows put a temporary halt to the Lysander's activities and a tragic accident put a full stop to Major Temple's life. One of the Partisan heroines described in tears how the brave major died.

Lucia Testori was born in Castelletto di Stura in the province of Cuneo in 1920. She worked with the anti-Fascists of that area from September, 1943, and was a guide to many different commanders of British missions in north-west Italy. Petite, with long dark brown hair and brown eyes, she was a fearless courier. She regularly pedalled her bicycle through enemy lines with plastic explosive strapped to her waist under her skirt. She told me of Major Temple's death round the Cisterna campfires one night and later provided this graphic eye-witness account.

'On the evening of 12 November, 1944, the Nazis and Fascists began an attack over a large area,' she said. 'They had considerable forces in the Langhe area, where in broad daylight much material had been parachuted to the Partisans. On 15 November, Ciglie Castle risked being encircled and the whole British mission boarded a small uncovered lorry. In the cabin there was the driver and the interpreter; in the back, unprotected, were myself, Temple and the other British members, seated on equipment.

'We set off towards Marsiglia, hearing the shells exploding ever closer. The enemy had broken our lines in several places. At Marsiglia Temple had a few things to do. He got down from the lorry and went to the storehouse of the First Langhe Division. When he came out, he was kept talking for some time by the Partisan commander.

'We remained on the lorry, anxious to set off again. Around us there was nobody left. It was about 10 am. Our lorry was parked at the corner of a square. On our left there was a stone wall and further on there was the beginning of a small street that sloped down around a corner leading out of the village.

'We called him several times, worried at the explosions which were coming ever nearer. The lorry began to move off slowly and Temple, who was agile and athletic despite his weight, managed to run to reach the left side of the lorry. He caught hold of the side with his hands and tried to jump inside. He remained outside next to the back wheel, unable to clamber over the edge as the lorry pulled forward. Suddenly a cart full of straw pulled by oxen came round the corner and our driver had to swerve left towards the stone wall. Temple was crushed between the wall and the side of the lorry. He twisted round twice and fell to the ground. Whenever I recall this incident, I can see again his eyes wide open with the pain.

'We took him to Murazzano. The hospital and indeed the whole town was in chaos, evacuating the wounded. Temple asked Mauri for news of the battle, and the latter gave us a car to continue to another hospital at Cortemilia, which was a safer place.

'Temple was in a serious condition. "Lussia" – for so he called me – "I am thirsty". These were now his only words. Every now and then we stopped to fill the water bottle.

'At the Cortemilia hospital they did everything possible to save him, but, despite their efforts, at 2 pm that same day, 15 November, 1944, he died of internal haemorrhaging.'

Major Temple's body was one of the last to be flown south that late autumn from the Vesime airstrip before winter closed down that particular route.

As Lucia told the story then, and whenever she has told it since, I have often pondered how some men seem to enjoy a charmed life for so long. But when their luck runs out it seems the fickle finger of fate has singled them out for misfortune.

Just as it was for Major Temple, so, I reflected, it had happened for the brave Captains Gubbins and Keany. Within the month the same cruel twist would snuff out the life of Major Hope.

But for now he was sitting in front of me, full of life and telling eagerly that all systems were working towards the large-scale emigration south of various Allies and wounded Partisans from Vesime.

The overall operation was being organized by Captain W.J. 'Jimmy' Sayers, a tall, slim, dark-moustachioed officer from the Royal Corps of Signals who had volunteered for the S.O.E. For much of the time I had been at Cisterna after Keany's death, Sayers had been trapped on the far side of the Tanaro, unable to cross because of the swollen river and enemy troop activities. But by 1 April he had reached the Vesime area and was making all the complex arrangements to time the completion of the runway with the arrival of the C-47 and the assembling of the evacuees. All this had to be done without attracting the unwelcome attention of the Fascists or their spies. We realized that this was nigh impossible, so we soaked the region with every disposable Partisan and gave strict instructions that nobody was to be allowed in or out of a three-mile radius of Vesime unless and until they had been thoroughly vetted.

I had a farewell glass of wine with Group Bombardier Basil 'Jack' Temple in what the Partisans regarded as a 'safe' bar in San Damiano. I had met him earlier when I passed through Cisterna with Captain Keany. At that time Temple was being sheltered in the town by Tino Cartello and his family. Before then the 23-year-old flying ace had been living in hay lofts throughout the harsh winter, surviving on a diet of polenta and sparrows which the Partisans netted and roasted.

'Not much meat on them but quite tasty,' he had remarked.

Before he was flown out of Vesime, Temple had been holed up in the comparative luxury of a tiny hotel in San Damiano, although largely confined to his room. He was excited by the prospect of being reunited with his colleagues – Co-Pilot Joe Rademacher, turret gunner Carl Raisig and tail gunner Frank McGrath.

Although he was aware that injured waist gunner Joe Glydon had been captured by the Germans, Temple did not know that navigator Mitchell and pilot Hacking had fallen into enemy hands. (Nor did Temple know he had become a father – his first child, Nancy, was born in the USA fourteen days after he was shot down).

As we slugged back our wine, while keeping a cautious eye open for Republican soldiers, Temple told me how local inhabitants had risked being shot and gone hungry to keep him alive while he was avoiding capture. His great fear was that the ending of the Second World War could be the start of civil conflict within Italy. He had obviously become fond of Piedmont and attached to its people, at least to those who were on our side.

On 2 April the preparations had all been made. Shortly after dawn the field had been transformed back into a landing strip. Temple, Rademacher, Raisig and McGrath were brought to the area to await their departure. The eight airmen who had made a forced landing at Turin were also delivered by their Partisan escorts to the makeshift 'departure lounge' in a hedgerow. If my memory serves, two escaped prisoners-of-war from Britain were also assembled to join the exodus, together with six wounded Partisans who needed urgent hospital treatment.

One of the last jobs of the team preparing the landing field was to chop down the solitary tree at the end of the upward slope. It was now reduced to a two-feet high stump. With chippings all around it, the freshly-hewn wood gleamed in the filtered sunlight as if to signal to the incoming plane that all was ready.

Right on time the C47 appeared in the sky. It circled once and then landed with nothing to spare at either end of the field. The pilot, a Captain Buchanan, signalled for his passengers to come over immediately. Those who were fit helped to carry and load the injured. Captain Buchanan did not waste a second but taxied straightaway to the furthest possible point at the end of the field. His tailfins were almost in the far hedge as he revved his engines and adjusted the flaps down to maximum for take-off lift.

The Captain released his brakes and the C47 began to pick up speed, agonisingly slowly. Half-way across the field we were convinced he would never make it. All the passengers had been loaded as far forward as possible for optimum weight distribution.

Temple was standing in the large double doorway normally used by parachutists. I could see the alarm in his eyes when, at the last moment before disaster, Buchanan wrenched the nose of the aircraft off the ground.

Temple told me later that as he looked out of the doorway they were so close to the tree stump that he could actually see the axe marks in the wood. He described it as one of the best feats of flying he had ever seen – and one he never wanted to see again from that position.

After clearing the first hurdle and avoiding the rise at the end of the field, Buchanan then had to drop the nose of his aircraft into a small valley beyond the mound and gain enough air speed to keep flying. Once that had been achieved, the rest of the journey back to the Allied base at Siena was, in R.A.F. lingo, a piece of cake!

IX

TRAGEDY AND LIBERATION

Back in Cisterna we were all feeling in an exalted mood over the success of the Vesime operation. There was much brave talk about what a pity it was that the Fascists had not turned up to provide us with target practice. But in the longer-term view of leaders like Otello and Hope, it was another encouraging sign of the enemy's fear.

We were in good voice that night, although my comrades were somewhat bemused when I gave them my stirring rendition of 'Soldiers of the King'. The Partisans were happy to join in the spirit of the song even if they did not understand one word they were mumbling. But they drew the line and drowned me out when I attempted an encore with 'What is the Meaning of Empire Day ?'

During the next few days the S.O.E. staff were kept busy with the ordering and receipt of arms and ammunition, which were now dropping like confetti around Cisterna. Long-term Partisans were already armed to the teeth, but new recruits were coming forward daily to join our cause and remove the hated Fascists from the last of Italy's northern cities.

As soon as we had a respite from these activities, I was given the opportunity to join another sabotage mission with the Bandits of Cisterna. This time the men from the 21st Brigade of the Autonomous Partisans at San Damiano were planning an attack on a railway viaduct at Villafranca. I knew the town well, I pretended, hoping I could swing myself the trip on the basis of my local knowledge. In fact my geographical expertise was limited to a mad dash through the town at night on a donkey and cart while Keany and I were dressed as peasants. But my bogus credentials were unnecessary. I was told that Dino Tartaglino had invited *'Biondino'* along. I was slightly more pleased by the offer than I was to know that my nickname had been changed from 'English Billy' to 'Blondie'.

I departed once more at dusk with Nino and another Partisan called Vincenzo. He was a taciturn guerrilla fighter who seemed to speak neither Italian nor English. Vincenzo spent the entire journey chain-smoking and communicating with both Nino and I by a series of grunts and expressive arm-waving or hand signals.

Nino explained en route that Vincenzo was not in possession of a complete set of marbles. But he had the heart of a lion and was totally devoted to the cause in general and Major Mauri in particular. He followed him with blind loyalty just as a contented dog would pursue its master to the ends of the earth.

Mauri had instructed Vincenzo to stay at Cisterna and follow the instructions of Otello. While it must have hurt the dedicated Partisan to lose sight of his adored leader, he would never question his decision. Now Nino and I were happy in the knowledge the Vincenzo had been instructed to take us safely to Villafranca. We knew he would not let Mauri down by failing in that task.

As midnight approached on a cool, clear evening, we rendezvoused with Tartaglino and his men as arranged. He greeted us enthusiastically and explained that Republican troops had pulled out of the town temporarily, following an attack by Partisans of the Justice and Liberty Party.

'Before they assemble a large force and return, we must blow the viaduct,' said the burly butcher with a handsome smile. 'It will take the Fascists two months to repair the damage and by then the war will be over.'

Tartaglino had obviously heard from Nino of my

unwarranted reputation as an explosives expert. It became apparent that he wanted to show me he had under his command two formidable demolition men of his own.

Nini Bellero, one of the sons of Gris and Grisa, and his comrade Luigi Chiavetta, a swarthy Sicilian from the 22nd Brigade, handled their deadly merchandise with as much confidence as a grocer handles packets of butter. I smiled confidently to hide my terror as they showed me by a combination of schoolboy Italian, pidgin English and sign language what they were proposing to do. Tartaglino looked on, beaming with pleasure, to see if I approved.

Bellero and Chiavetta were proposing to blow up one arch of a stretch of viaduct, and they intended to concentrate all their explosive power on that one target. There was nothing in my limited knowledge of the subject for me to take exception to this course of action so I nodded enthusiastically to demonstrate my approval. They had collected eighty pieces of plastic and gun cotton explosive which they were planting and draping over strategic points in the arch. The pair of them also had some phosphorus fire bombs which they hoped would ignite the railway sleepers, causing further damage which would require large sections of track to be removed.

Unhappily these ancillary incendiary devices nearly wrecked the whole spectacular operation. After Bellero and Chiavetta had completed the placings of the explosives and prepared to set the fuse, one of the phosphorus bombs somehow burst alight. Without a word or a moment's hesitation, both men dived on it and smothered the flames with their clothing. They were unharmed, as they quickly tore off their smouldering jackets, and the danger had ended as suddenly as it had begun. But it reminded all concerned of the volatile nature of the substances we were using.

They set a ten-minute delay fuse to their complex firework display and we scampered away to take up position some 500 yards distant. The subsequent blasts were every bit as good as my own effort with the goods train. As one series of explosions blew out key sections of the arch at its crucial stress points, a larger rumbling noise at its base indicated the weakening of its support. The phosphorus bombs then burst into life to illuminate the scene on a more permanent basis as the arch gave up the unequal struggle. With what sounded like a giant's sigh, it disintegrated in slow motion before our eyes and collapsed in a cloud of dust and rubble. The track came down for thirty yards on either side and parts of it dangled into the newly-created chasm. When all the noise had ceased and the dust had settled, the viaduct looked like a set of teeth with one missing.

For once Partisan discipline failed and we all let out a mighty cheer. But after that momentary lapse we returned to silence, shook hands, clasped shoulders and went our separate ways.

On the farm tracks and lanes leading back to Cisterna, Vincenzo was beside himself with joy. He kept chuckling, mouthing the word 'Boom' and then giving an animated mime impression of a railway arch disappearing. From the way he kept smiling at me, I could tell he thought I had somehow masterminded the whole thing. I blush when I write that I said nothing to discourage his high opinion of me.

A week later I was back in action again, this time supporting the 6th Division of the Partisans' Asti Brigade when they ambushed a column of German and Republican troops. It happened when Mauri's men had been occupying the town of Alba for two days. As he had anticipated, the enemy sent reinforcements to support their demoralized forces and push the Partisans out of the town.

The Axis powers must have thought they were taking no chances when they sent two armoured cars and three light tanks to precede a column of some 200 Fascist soldiers out of Bra, but they were blissfully unaware of the extent to which S.O.E. had supplied their opponents.

We brought further supplies to the newest recruits as they waited to ambush the column north of Alba on the left bank of the Tanaro. Major Mauri was a master strategist and he had taken the town for this very purpose. Instead of concentrating his men in Alba to defend his prize, he had sent the main body to join in the attack on the unsuspecting

German and Italian soldiers. With an ample supply of machine guns and mortars they made mincemeat of the opposition.

I was too far behind the front line — I was learning the value of caution — to see exactly what was happening as our guns opened up on them. There was a thunderous noise and a cloud of smoke hung like a pall over the proceedings.

But at the end of the day, with the Fascists fleeing back to Bra with their tails between their legs, they had lost fifteen dead and twenty wounded. Two armoured cars had been destroyed. In contrast, none of the Partisans had suffered so much as a scratch. We were enjoying one heady success after another. I suppose it was inevitable that tragedy would strike to remind us of our fallibility and our mortality.

On 17 April we had supervised what was now becoming a routine supply drop at Cisterna. Partisans and S.O.E. men had assisted in the positioning of straw bales for signal fires and the distribution of paraffin. All the appropriate arrangements had been made for two Dakotas to appear at about 10 pm.

I flashed the agreed Morse letters with my torch and the planes disgorged their cargoes. They landed in a field a mile from the castle. Some fifty Partisans were assisting with the collections that night, but there was only one container which interested Millard and me. For some weeks we had run out of our beloved English cigarettes. Two Italian brands were also in short supply. The ones called 'Nazionale' were appalling. The other brand, 'Populare', were even worse. As heavy smokers, Millard and I would try anything to feed our habit. In desperation I had even rolled up dried leaves on one occasion to satisfy the craving for a fag. But on this night I knew we were in line for what was known as a 'comforts' parcel. This was to include several cartons of Gold Flake cigarettes.

Like two heroin addicts waiting for their next fix, Millard and I scanned the skies for the cigar-tube-shaped container wrapped in a distinctive red ribbon. As far as we were concerned, the Partisans could help themselves to any weapons or ammo they liked. But they were not getting their hands on the S.O.E. goodie bag.

'There it is,' shouted Millard, whose eyesight was as sharp as a hawk on occasions such as these. Without further ado I set off in the direction of his pointing finger, with Busty hot on my heels. We arrived ahead of the Partisan pack and proceeded to carry our treasure back to Cisterna. Although I would have trusted my fellow bandits with my life, I would not have trusted them with our Gold Flake cigarettes.

Millard and I savoured the moment like a couple of connoisseurs as the smoke was sucked into our lungs and slowly exhaled. Then we filled our pockets with cartons and our mouths with chocolate like naughty schoolboys.

Hope and Otello were supervising the unloading proceedings and they chose to overlook the missing items which had already been purloined by Millard and I. We were treated to a knowing look, but nothing was said.

The Partisans were excited and happy with their latest weaponry windfall, which was more than enough to equip their growing army of recruits. After the supplies had been stashed away, we all trooped across to a meeting hall, which may have been the local school assembly room, where we held a celebration party. Red wine was flowing as we stood on the wooden floorboards eating chocolates and puffing away contentedly at our Gold Flakes. It had been a long day and by 11.30 pm Millard and I were ready to turn in for the night. It was a source of irritation to me that we should be confined to a smelly shippon while Major Hope and Captain Roccia enjoyed the luxury of a farmhouse billet.

'That's one of the privileges of rank,' Busty pointed out as I complained bitterly on the way back to our quarters. I had earlier bade the Major a rather frosty 'Good night' when he told me I had been allocated the cattle shed once again.

Millard and I walked 400 yards to our shippon and were just bedding down for the night when a Partisan rushed in and shouted, 'Come quickly. Major Hope has been shot.'

I ran down the road with Millard back to the meeting hall where we had parted five minutes earlier. The Major, still wearing his battledress, was lying motionless on the floor.

His eyes were shut and I soon established from the lack of pulse or heartbeat that he was dead. Roccia was wringing his hands in agony, fighting back tears and wailing, 'What are we going to do? What are we going to do ?'

Surprisingly there was no sign of blood. The Major had a small hole in his stomach where a bullet had entered and another where it had exited through his back. When I helped Millard lift him on to a table, I was surprised to hear the bones crack in his legs. Apparently this is a common phenomenon among corpses.

As I laid out Hope's body I asked Roccia what had happened. His voice was trembling with emotion as he explained how Hope had died as a result of the unluckiest of freak accidents. The party was drawing to a close just before midnight and people were bidding each other good night. As one of the Partisans reached out to shake Major Hope's hand, a shot rang out. A marshal from the Carabinieri named Pasquale Bolle was the unfortunate Partisan responsible. As he extended his hand and said 'Good night,' the sten gun slipped off his shoulder and clattered to the floor.

Bolle must have had a bullet up the spout and the safety catch in the 'off' position. Even so it was a million to one chance that the weapon would fall to the floor in such a way that the trigger would be activated. The odds must also have been long against the single bullet discharged striking one of Hope's vital organs. Nevertheless half-a-dozen witnesses saw that that was exactly what had happened. The bullet pierced Hope's liver and one kidney. He died almost instantly. Bolle was in tears as Roccia told me the story. With his head in his hands Bolle kept repeating 'Sorry' and 'Accident' over and over again.

Within a few minutes an Italian doctor arrived on the scene to tell us what we already knew — that Hope was dead. Major Ballard had been summoned and he came to the hall to warn me to keep my eyes and ears open.

Ballard and Hope were fellow South Africans and Ballard regarded the incident as highly suspicious. It certainly was the most unlikely accident, but I am convinced it happened as Roccia described. For a start the Partisans had no reason to want Hope killed. He had done them proud in the supply of arms for the past two months, especially that night. Furthermore there were many convincing witnesses who confirmed Bolle's story. And who would invent such an incredible version of events if they were covering up a murder?

We took Hope's body to the Roman Catholic church in Cisterna in the early hours of the following morning. His corpse, still in uniform and draped with a Union Jack, lay in an open coffin overnight with a formal guard of honour. Millard and I shared this duty with two runaway prisoners who had been fighting alongside the Partisans and had just arrived in Cisterna. One was a Geordie lad who had been a private in the Durham Light Infantry. The other was a Liverpuddlian who had served as a gunner with the Royal Artillery. They told me how they had lived in the mountains with a group of fellow prison runaways who had taken to the hills. They had fled when the Italian Government of Marshal Badoglio surrendered in September, 1943, and their guards opened the camp gates. But when the Germans and Mussolini rescinded that surrender, they all became wanted men.

Many hid out in the hillsides, living off the land, stealing from the farmers, and making themselves extremely unpopular with their rural neighbours. Some gave themselves up to become prisoners-of-war again. Others were recaptured during the *rastrellamenti*. These two had decided to link up with the Partisans and had fought alongside them for many months before their recent arrival at the castle.

Now, in the tattered remnants of their uniforms, they made an untidy guard of honour, standing to attention in a candlelit vigil by the side of Hope's open coffin in front of the altar.

The following morning a priest officiated at a special service for Major Hope, and Partisans from miles around flocked to the funeral to pay their respects to the man with the strange accent who had helped them to fight Fascism on equal terms.

As the coffin was sealed in a wall of the church graveyard, Major Ballard gave a moving speech about their South African homeland. With tears filling his eyes, the Major spoke of the day their spirits would meet once again across the Veldt. Few of the Partisans could understand a word he was saying, but the raw emotion of his message was clear enough to any man.

Major Mauri attended the funeral and afterwards he announced to the mourners that henceforth the 6th Alpine Asti division which covered the Cisterna area would be renamed the 'Major Hope Division' in his memory. The anti-Fascists had good reason to be grateful to Hope and to mourn his passing, especially in view of the tragic manner of his death at their hands.

The previous night's drop of arms and ammunition meant that the Major had achieved his personal target of providing the Autonomous Partisans with all the weapon power they needed. As a result of his efforts they now had: seven heavy and twenty light machine guns; three bazookas and two Projectile Infantry Anti-Tank weapons (known as PIATs, the British equivalent of the American bazooka); one mortar and one small artillery cannon; 180 rifles and pistols; boxes of hand grenades, a large quantity of plastic explosives and countless rounds of ammunition.

It is interesting to note statistics which show how the Partisan strength had grown in the area by studying the records of the 21st (San Damiano) Brigade. On 8 August, 1944, they had twenty men armed with a heavy machine gun, six stens and twenty-six rifles. By September their membership had doubled. In December there were ninety of them. By January their numbers had risen to 115 and the following month there were 160. When Hope was shot, the San Damiano brigade had swollen to 225 men, a combination of battle-hardened guerrilla fighters and raw but enthusiastic recruits.

After the funeral Mauri talked strategy and tactics with Otello, Roccia and myself. Although a lowly sergeant, I was now a key figure in the operation as the man who got the messages in and out of the area.

Mauri and Otello sensed that the time was ripe to attack Asti. They had heard rumours for more than a month that the Germans had pulled out of the city leaving the Italian Republican soldiers to keep order and the Fascist flag flying. Now they were receiving reports that these soldiers would flee at the first sign of a concerted Partisan move towards Asti.

Roccia was alarmed to hear the way Mauri and Otello were talking. The Allies had told their Partisan colleagues that they were unable to advance north from the Gothic Line during the winter months. They urged the Partisans to hold their positions as best they could, to carry out harrying sabotage missions and guerrilla raids and to await the Allied advance. But the Partisans were in no mood to heed this directive. They were like eager gun-dogs straining at the leash. They had suffered thousands of casualties as a result of Fascist attacks and *rastrellamenti*, as well as denouncements by spies and double agents. Mauri and Otello argued that they had neither the power nor the inclination to hold their men back now the sweet smell of success was in their nostrils after so much hardship and deprivation.

Roccia was in a dilemma. As an Italian he fully understood their feelings and emotions. As a British officer it was his duty to obey the official line and to discourage any suggestion of independent action by the Partisans. With a divided conscience he could be forgiven for dithering over both sides of the argument.

On 22 April I received an unequivocal message from Field-Marshal Alexander of Tunis. The order was meant for Roccia, to pass on to Otello, but I translated it myself from code and told the Partisan leader directly.

The Field-Marshal, informed by Roccia of the Partisans' likely intentions, was ordering them under no circumstances to attack the major northern cities until the Allies arrived to lead them. I kept a perfectly deadpan face as I informed Otello of this directive. But I could not help smiling when, in the most colourful language, Otello told me what my Field-Marshal could do with his orders.

The 6th Alpine (Asti-Major Hope) Division alone had lost twenty-nine dead and 167 wounded to reach this moment. They would not and should not be denied their hour of glory, said Otello. Even more powerfully, he insisted that if his politically neutral force did not move in to fill the vacuum caused by the evaporating Fascists, then it would be occupied by the Communist Garibaldini.

'The people will welcome liberation by anyone,' said Otello. 'If the Communists get there first, they will be hard to budge.'

I could see the perfect sense in this remark, even if my superiors at base H.Q. could not. Besides, I was one of the Bandits of Cisterna myself now and I knew how important it was to my comrades to enjoy their triumph.

'What will the Allies do, Biondino, if we ignore their order?' asked Otello.

'Not a lot they can do really, is there?' I replied.

'Exactly,' said Otello, grinning wolfishly.

Roccia was now in a flat spin, knowing that a Field-Marshal's orders were about to be defied. But there was nothing we could do about it.

'We can't beat 'em so we might as well join 'em,' was my advice. Eventually Roccia agreed it was better to be with the Partisans when they moved forward than to stay in Cisterna wailing and gnashing our teeth.

By 24 April intelligence was reaching fever pitch from all our sources that the Germans had long departed Asti. We also heard that most of the Italian Republican officers had gone with them and now dozens of ordinary Fascist soldiers were discarding their uniforms to join the cries of 'Death to Mussolini'.

Otello had been advised by Mauri to advance on Asti when he judged the time was right. Otello stayed behind in Cisterna but despatched a force of some 200 men to march the four miles to San Damiano.

We were led by Dino Tartaglino. I dusted down my crumpled battledress, gave my boots some semblance of a shine and marched alongside him. I was also wearing my paratroopers' red beret. (This had been grudgingly given to me at Monopoli and I had smuggled it out with me when we flew from Cecina eleven weeks earlier). I felt proud once more to be a member of the British Army. I was also proud to be marching towards a free world with this ragged bunch of heroes.

Millard was wearing a black beret with his battledress and Roccia joined us at the head of the procession from Cisterna to San Damiano. Our information was correct and there was no sign of opposition as we entered San Damiano.

Townsfolk were cheering and dancing in the streets when we arrived in the main square. After pausing for a little food and a lot of drink, Tartaglino decided we should press on that same night for Asti. He had heard that other rival groups of Partisans were heading in that direction.

A convoy of vehicles was requisitioned and we headed for the city four miles away. It was a joyous occasion as we rattled about in a bone-jarring lorry singing favourite songs like 'We Partisans of the Woods' and 'When the Time Comes to Shoot We Partisans are Always First'. I think I even got them to join me in 'Rule Britannia'.

The 200 of us arrived on the outskirts of Asti at dawn. Units from the Garibaldini and the Justice and Liberty group from Cinaglio were already assembling their forces when we turned up on the scene. Happily there was no discord among the rival factions as we were still unsure of the Fascist resistance we might have to overcome together.

Tartaglino immediately ordered his men to march forward on foot. I fell in alongside him. I was made to feel like the conquering hero as we stepped through the gates of the city. The cheering crowd was ten deep on either side of the street as we started to troop forward. Our speed slackened to a saunter to accommodate the girls and women who kept rushing forward, hugging us and planting kisses on our cheeks. The green, white and red flags of Italy were flying and being waved everywhere. Material from curtains and tablecloths had been used to make them. I also spotted several Union Jacks fluttering from the rooftops in recognition of the part we had played.

As we headed for the city hall, the roar of a plane was heard overhead. Instinctively we all cowered momentarily at the possibility of a spiteful enemy aircraft aiming to spoil the party. But I soon recognized the R.A.F. markings on the familiar structure of a good old Spitfire. The lone aircraft carried out a perfect victory roll as it passed over the main streets of the city at low altitude. Then it waggled its wings as it departed as a final salute.

There was no resistance to our march into the city, although I saw some of the crowd dragging away suspected Fascists for retribution. They were protesting their innocence and begging for mercy. I later heard that most of these men were roughed up and some were subsequently charged with war crimes.

Young women who had associated with Fascist soldiers were also getting their day of reckoning. Despite their tears and struggles, they were held down while amateur barbers cut off all their hair. Then their near-bald heads were painted red so all could see their shame.

Meanwhile we were being handed jugs, bottles, flasks and pouches of wine as our triumphant march through the streets started to deteriorate into a mobile party. When we reached the steps of the city hall there was a slight delay while the new officials were installed. Then Tartaglino and I walked up to greet the incumbent prefect. His eyes were brimming with emotion as he clasped Dino to his bosom, patted his back and kissed him on both cheeks. Then it was my turn. I would have appreciated the gesture more if he had bothered to shave that morning.

After the official liberation ceremony was over, the crowds surged forward and mobbed us. Pretty girls were showering us with kisses and complete strangers were pressing drinks into our hands. We protested of course, but resistance was impossible. We had no alternative but to acquiesce.

On that joyful night of 25 April in Asti, Roccia, Millard and I were joined by a new S.O.E. captain called Powell. He told me that he and his senior officer, Major Leach, had been flown in to replace Hope. I believe they had landed by Lysander at Vesime. We explained to him that trying to stop the Partisans from liberating their local city had been like King Canute's effort to stem the tide. We had accompanied them into Asti to ensure an Allied presence on Liberation

Day. Powell seemed perfectly happy that we had bowed to the inevitable.

When I told him that vehicles were being requisitioned, even as we spoke, to head north for the liberation of Turin, Powell simply shrugged.

'If it's going to happen anyway, we might as well be there,' he said. It seemed to me that the S.O.E. were taking a more realistic view of events than Army G.H.Q.

In Asti I was also reunited with a fellow radio operator I had last seen at the training base in Monopoli. Corporal 'Shady' Lane was a Londoner, one of two men called Lane who had worked with me. The other had the misfortune to be given the nickname 'Lola' after a Hollywood film star of that era.

Lane and I hopped into one of the lorries which the Partisans had commandeered and joined the convoy for Turin. After 20 miles we reached a suburb called Superga, which was later to earn post-war notoriety as the spot where the Turin soccer team perished in an air crash. Our convoy arrived on 26 April and I immediately saw signs of fighting. Just outside our billet was a garden where the Partisans had made a half-hearted attempt to bury some of the Fascist victims. In six shallow graves the arms and legs of the soldiers' bodies were sticking out of the freshly-dug soil.

Major Mauri was in Turin to lead his men into the city. With him were the 6th Asti Division, 'Belbo' brigade of the 2nd Langhe Division, and the second brigade of the 1st Langhe Division as well as the units from the 6th Alpine (Asti-Major Hope) Division which I had adopted. It was the morning of 27 April when Mauri led his tattered troops of freedom fighters into that famous north Italian city to end years of Fascist tyranny.

Unlike the carnival atmosphere of Asti, the streets of Turin were empty. Pockets of resistance had to be destroyed as the Partisans became involved in house-to-house fighting. The bodies of Republican soldiers were lying in the streets where they had fallen. One was hanging from a lamppost.

I had left Millard in charge of the radio at Superga while I aimed for the city centre with Shady Lane and the legendary guerrilla leader Gris and his three sons. We took up firing positions and ran from corner to corner, archway to archway, block to block, as Fascist diehards took potshots at us from the tall buildings. Other Partisans joined us in shooting in the direction of the sniper fire. Occasionally a figure would fall crashing from the rooftops, but none of us could tell for certain who had been the successful marksman.

To vary the angle of attack and make life more precarious for us, from time to time a car would flash by with a Republican soldier firing a machine gun out of its window. It reminded me of scenes from gangster movies, but these were real bullets pinging into the brickwork behind us and we would fling ourselves into shop doorways until the danger had passed.

Gradually the shootings petered out and civilians started to emerge at their windows, smiling cautiously. As their courage returned they waved and cheered at us until the scene resembled that in Asti.

Mauri and his men fought their way through the Colline del Pino (Pine Valley) and entered the Piazza Castello (Castle Square) to hoist the Italian flag to symbolize the liberation of Turin. During that final skirmishing, thirty-five more Fascists were killed and a further nineteen wounded. The Partisans lost three dead and six wounded.

My final memory of that historic day came as the Italian flag was being raised. A smartly-dressed Englishwoman of about 35 emerged from the shadows and spoke to me in impeccable English. She was wearing a two-piece suit which sported a hand-embroidered Union Jack on its sleeve.

Recognizing my uniform, she flung her arms round me and said, 'You're English aren't you? Where are all the others?'

I said, 'They're on their way. We're the first to arrive.'

Then this mysterious lady stepped back into the shadows, turned and smiled. 'Thank God. It's all over then,' she said and disappeared.

EPILOGUE

I never did solve the mystery of the intriguing Englishwoman in Turin. She disappeared as quickly as she had
materialized and I have not seen her since. The next day
forward elements of a South African regiment arrived in
the liberated city. They were followed by American
soldiers as the war in Europe was heading for a swift conclusion.

We spent the next six weeks in Turin, running a signals
station from a beautiful villa at Superga, owned by Signor
Agnelli, boss of the Fiat car company. Shady Lane, Bill
Beggs and I also made frequent tours of the city's nightlife,
a study which often resulted in the three of us sleeping it
off on a billiard table in the basement of our favourite bar.

From Turin I set off for Siena, making a slight diversion
to Monesiglio on the way. There I collected two dressing
gowns and four pairs of pyjamas which the tailoress had
made as promised for Keany and myself from our parachutes. On my arrival in Siena I was given a week's leave at a
rest camp in Rome.

Before taking that break I applied to be dropped behind
enemy lines again. This time I volunteered to go to Cey-
lon, from where agents were parachuted into Japanese-held
territory in Malaya. But a couple of atomic bombs on
Hiroshima and Nagasaki put an end to hostilities before
my request could even be considered.

As soon as the war with Japan was over, the S.O.E. was
disbanded and I was moved to the Royal Signals base
depot at Naples.

On 25 October, 1945, the *London Gazette* announced I
had been awarded the Military Medal for 'bravery in the
field'. The following month, during a spell of home leave

in Manchester, I received a letter of confirmation from Major Alan Clarke and the congratulations of General Colin Gubbins for my decoration. The citation read as follows:

MILITARY MEDAL
Sgt. William Arthur Pickering, R. Sigs

Sgt Pickering was parachuted into SOUTH PIEDMONT on 4 Feb 45 in company with the senior British representative to the CLNAI. After about 10 days in the LANGHE area during which time the party was continually chased by GERMAN troops, Sgt PICKERING, in company with one of the officers of this mission, set out in an attempt to reach the neighbourhood of BRUSASCO. They moved constantly through enemy-infested country until they reached the area of MONTAFIA when they were again subjected to an enemy drive. On 8 Mar 45, they were forced to hide with a small partisan party on a hill in this area. Here they were attacked by the enemy in force and in the course of this action the officer with Sgt PICKERING was killed together with 4 partisans and the rest of the party was forced to withdraw. Sgt PICKERING risked his own life by continuing to carry the WT set which he succeeded in saving from falling into enemy hands.

Sgt PICKERING remained in the area until he could recover the body of his officer and arrange for its burial. After that he made his way back through enemy infested country to join up with another British mission at CISTERNA.

I was told I would be notified of when I was to travel to Buckingham Palace to receive my medal from George VI, but eventually it arrived in the post with a letter of apology from the King saying he was sorry he could not pin it upon me personally.

In the meantime I had been back in Italy, where I was posted to Florence in the company of an S.O.E. radio officer named Sergeant-Major Jock Campbell. He had been fighting with the Partisans in Yugoslavia alongside Brigadier Fitzroy MacLean and Major Randolph Churchill, son of Winston. Campbell described Churchill Junior as a 'pompous oaf — but incredibly brave to the point of folly.'

The Sergeant-Major shared my anarchic views of army discipline and we were caught off limits twice by the MPs before we arrived in Florence two weeks late following a few unofficial sightseeing trips. We were 'severely admonished' for our sins by Major 'Inky' Udell when, belatedly, we reached our destination.

It was in Florence that I met a beautiful signorina named Rossana Reboli. She was with her mother at a New Year's Eve dance in the sergeants' mess at the Villa San Camillo. By the time I was posted back to Rome in March, 1946, we had become engaged. I visited her again after being demobbed in 1947 and in October of that year we were married at St Chad's Roman Catholic Church in Cheadle, Cheshire.

Our son David was born in September, 1964. 'Rosa' and I are living at the time of writing in a bungalow in Hindley Green, near Wigan, Lancs, which we have named 'San Camillo'.

After I left the army I worked as a stores clerk and a fireman before going into business as a grocer with various shops around the Manchester area. In 1981 I was appointed area manager of the Oxfam charity's retail outlets and I was responsible for the finding and staffing of shops throughout the North West until my retirement in 1988.

I have served in the Army Cadet Force for 40 years, reaching the rank of major, and I am secretary of the Manchester branch of the Royal Regiment of Wales Old Comrades Association. I am also a member of the Greater Manchester Army Cadet Force Welfare Committee and the Special Forces Club.

But my greatest pleasure in life is to return to those hills in Piedmont for reunions with a dwindling band of ageing friends — the Bandits of Cisterna.

During these merry meetings I have learned a great deal more about the political significance of our war effort than I ever realized at the time I was fighting. Much of the credit for that belongs to Major Massimo 'Max' Salvadori, who had managed not only to survive but thrive in Milan despite the ill-fated mission of Keany and I to reach him there. Salvadori, who had already won the Military Cross for his heroism at Anzio, where he was wounded, was awarded the Distinguished Service Order for his work in coordinating the efforts of the local resistance groups.

At a 1989 reunion in Piedmont Salvadori described how the struggles and sacrifices of the Partisans had ensured an orderly takeover of Milan which had helped to avert two distinct threats. One was that the defeat of the Germans and the disintegration of the R.S.I. (Repubblica Sociale Italiana) was not followed by a free-for-all in which the strongest would triumph. The second was avoiding the occupation of the Val d'Aosta and other western valleys by the Gaullists and the seizing of eastern Venetia by Titoists.

It was only when Salvadori explained these dangers 44 years later that I realized for the first time that our forays and adventures had perhaps played a part in preventing areas of Italy becoming regarded as the spoils of war.

Readers may be interested to know what became of some of my comrades at the end of the war.

Major Max Salvadori emigrated to the U.S.A., where he became Professor of Modern European history at Smith College, Massachusetts. He has written many books on the resistance which were published in Italy.

Captain Corbett, who gave me my first promotion in North Africa, was elected Mayor of Bebbington on The Wirral, Cheshire. He died in France in 1978.

Major Malcolm Munthe never fought again after being wounded at Anzio. He was invalided out of the army and went to live in Italy with his family at the end of the war.

Captain Charles Mackintosh, who accompanied me through Sicily, went on to organize safe passages through enemy lines for escaping prisoners of war in Italy. He was awarded the Distinguished Service Order. After the war, Mackintosh worked for the Shell Oil Company and retired in 1971 as president of their Spanish section. He died in 1979.

Captain Dick Cooper, who hypnotised me in Naples during our Christmas celebrations, wrote several books about his exploits, including one appropriately entitled *Born to Fight*.

Sergeant Denis McDonnell, who was also with me in Sicily, went on to work as a postman in his native Scotland. He returned to live in Balloch, on the bonny, bonny banks of Loch Lomond.

Sergeant Frank Gee, who worked with the S.O.E. in Naples, became a town councillor in Sale, Cheshire.

Adrian Gallegos, who took agents from the island of Ischia to their dropping points, was captured twice while working for the S.O.E. He escaped on both occasions and retired to Spain.

Alberto Tarchiani, who accompanied our group to Anzio, became the Italian Ambassador to the U.S.A. at the end of the war.

Jock Shannon, who trained with me at Henley and took the collections for my piano-playing, was presumed killed in action. He had dropped into enemy-held territory to link up with the resistance and was never heard from or seen again, a fate suffered by many of our S.O.E. agents.

Billy Beggs, who shared our good fortune in the 'wine liberation' escapade, and who rejoined me in Turin for further refreshing evenings, went on to become an assistant chief fire officer with the Lancashire County Brigade before his death in 1987.

Major Enrico Mauri, leader of the Alpine Division of the Partisans, was awarded the Medaglio D'Oro (Gold Medal) for his courage in organizing the resistance to the Fascists in the Langhe region. He and his toddler grandson were killed tragically in 1976 when their holiday plane crashed into a Greek mountainside. Major Mauri, aged 55, was one of 125 victims of the air disaster.

Giacomo Bagnasco, the teenage giant who met our landing party and the man I still suspect of stealing our cigarette rations, was working as a veterinary surgeon in Piedmont in 1990.

Captain Hugh Ballard, who spoke during Major Hope's

funeral service of meeting him again in the Veldt, died in South Africa after the war.

Colonel Toselli, the shrewd tactician known as 'Otello' who master-minded the defeat of the Fascists at Cisterna, was killed in a car crash in October, 1971. He and his wife, Signora Maria Romano Toselli, both died when the car he was driving came off the Turin motorway at Santena and hit a tree.

'Tal' Biestro, who had given food and shelter to Keany and I at Monesiglio, died in the late seventies when he fell from a hay loft and broke his neck.

His widow, Luisa Biestro, was still alive in 1990. After Tal's death she sold the farm and retired to Casale Monferrato.

Captain Luigi Cavalieri, alias Roccia, who was a member of the Operation Chariton team, returned to his legal practice in Rome where he became a successful lawyer.

Settimo Maggiorini, the fearless courier with the white beret and the red bike, became a Regimental Sergeant-Major with his beloved Alpini Regiment. He was still going strong in 1990, a sprightly 77-year-old living in Mondovi, tending his gardens and making his own wine.

Pietro Berutti, who guided us across the Tanaro on the rope-pulled boat, runs a world-renowned vineyard on the banks of the river at Barbaresco with his wife Romana. Their wine from 'La Spinosa' has won prizes for its quality in international competition.

Colonel Sir Douglas Dodds-Parker, who allowed me to stay in the S.O.E. after my drunken insults to the officers in North Africa, went on to become Tory M.P. for Cheltenham. He is a past president of the Special Forces Club in London.

Group Bombardier Basil 'Jack' Temple, who escaped with his American airmen colleagues from the makeshift landing strip at Vesime, returned to Kansas and saw his daughter Nancy, who had been born a fortnight after he was shot down in November, 1944. He had two more daughters and worked for a hardware company near New Orleans, where he became vice president.

Captain Jimmy Sayers, who played the major role in organizing the evacuation from Vesime, went on to fight in the Far East with Force 136. He took part in Operation Character in the Karen Hills for ten weeks prior to the Japanese surrender. He was demobbed in 1947 with the rank of Major and returned to Oxford University.

Lucia Boetto Testori, the courier who hid explosives under her skirt, was decorated with the *Medaglia di Bronzo al valor militare* with the *croce di guerra* (Bronze medal and Cross of War). Aged 70, she attended a reunion with S.O.E. representatives in London in 1990. She is a housewife and lives in Turin.

INDEX